When Did God Become a Christian?

DAVID KALAS

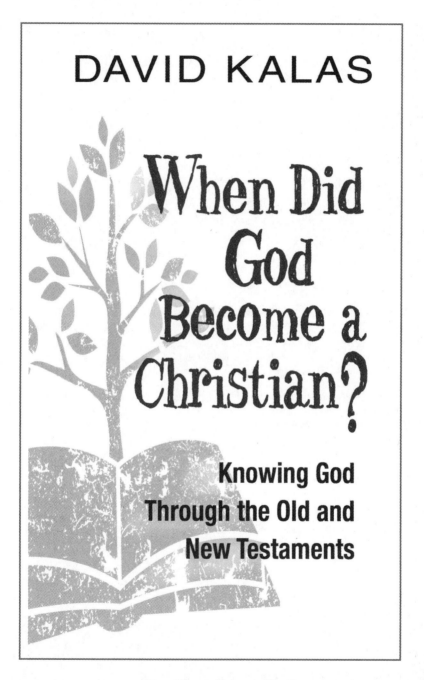

When Did God Become a Christian?

Knowing God Through the Old and New Testaments

Abingdon Press / Nashville

WHEN DID GOD BECOME A CHRISTIAN?
Knowing God Through the Old and New Testaments

This book is printed on elemental chlorine-free paper.

Library of Congress Cataloging-in-Publication data applied for.

ISBN 978-1-5018-3096-9

17 18 19 20 21 22 23 24 25 26 — 10 9 8 7 6 5 4 3 2 1

MANUFACTURED IN THE UNITED STATES OF AMERICA

To my father,
whose preaching brought the Bible to life,
and whose living made the Bible ring true.

Contents

Introduction 9

1. The Rumor Going Around the Church 11
   Unpacking a Common Question

2. Nothing New Under the Sun 19
   Gaining Some Historical Perspective

3. The Write-In Candidate 27
   Affirming the Unity of Scripture

4. Out on a Limb with a Saw 39
   Affirming the Reliability of Scripture

5. Israel's Home Movies 49
   Getting a Clearer Picture of God

6. A God at Odds? 59
   Clarifying the Integrity of God's Nature

7. Holy, Holy, Holy 67
   Seeing God's Holiness in the Old and New Testaments

8. Jesus Loves Me, This I Know 79
   Seeing God's Love in the Old and New Testaments

9. Finding True Love 97
   Exploring a Few Scriptures that Can Confuse Us

10. Heaven's Mission Statement 109
    Identifying the Continuity of God's Purpose and Plan

11. Same God, Different People 123
    Recognizing Who Has Changed

12. Nothing New About the Sun 139
    Considering How an Eternal God Is Unchanging

Notes 155

Introduction

As a youth minister, a pastor, and a preacher, I have had opportunities to teach the Bible to children, youth, and adults in a great variety of settings over the past thirty-five years. I can't think of a greater privilege. And in those hundreds and hundreds of settings where folks have been reading and discussing the Bible together, I've been asked a lot of questions. Perhaps the most common question is this: "When did God become a Christian?"

No one has actually asked it in exactly those words. Instead, that question has been asked in a dozen or more different ways. It comes as a question about why God commanded the Israelites "Thou shalt not kill" but then ordered them to conquer and slaughter whole nations. It comes as a question about the death penalty for adultery in the Old Testament Law compared to Jesus' choice not to condemn an adulterous woman in the New Testament. It is questions about Achan and Uzzah, Nadab and Abihu, and other stories that startle us and trouble our sensibilities. It is questions about genuinely questionable people whom God seems to accept and use, as well as other folks whom God destroys even though they don't seem so bad to us.

You and I rely on the Bible as the record of God's self-revelation, yet sometimes we struggle with how the Bible portrays God. Specifically, we struggle with depictions that seem incongruous with God's love.

I have written this book to assist us in those struggles. I do not intend to dismiss or explain away anything in Scripture. Rather, I proceed with the confidence that God's nature is unchanging, that God's love is perfect, and that God's written word is reliable. And so my endeavor is to help us understand the Bible more clearly in order that we might know God and his love more fully.

> I am so glad that my Father in heav'n
> Tells of His love in the Book He has giv'n,
> Wonderful things in the Bible I see;
> This is the dearest, that Jesus loves me.
>
> Philip P. Bliss, 1870

1

The Rumor Going
Around the Church

Unpacking a Common Question

Have you heard what people are saying about God? There is a rumor going around, one that I've heard often. In my years of being a parish pastor—serving in churches with both conservative and liberal leanings, in rural communities, in small towns, and in larger cities in several different states—I have heard the same rumor in every place. It does not seem to be confined to a region or limited to a demographic group. It is, in my experience, a remarkably—even frighteningly— pervasive rumor.

Most rumors, of course, are fairly localized. What may be a significant matter in one church in one community would be altogether irrelevant to a different church from another community. But this particular rumor seems to be widespread in churches all over the map.

It is a rumor about God. And the fact that it is about God means that the stakes are very high—especially if it's an inaccurate one.

Here's the rumor: *The God of the Old Testament is different from the God of the New Testament.*

Have you heard this rumor? Maybe even believed it? We want to evaluate that claim together.

In order to unpack some of our own personal feelings on this issue, let me invite you to conduct a simple experiment within the confines of your mind. Below are pairs of words suggestive of the two testaments. Read the words one at a time and consider the following: What comes to mind when you read each word? What sort of picture or image does each one inspire? Bear in mind that it takes only a moment to read the words and react to them, but if you can, allow extra time in each case to stop and examine your immediate reaction, taking a good look at the picture in your mind that represents each word before moving on to the next one.

Law
Gospel

Jehovah
Jesus

Old
New

Circumcision
Baptism

Prophets
Apostles

Passover
Communion

Did you notice a difference in the pictures that came to mind for each pair of words? Yes, the words are suggestive of the two testaments, but they are neutral. They are not loaded terms that carry strong negative or positive connotations. But you may have found that you liked some of the images these words evoked much better than others.

Meanwhile, there is one more pair of words that might be helpful for us to consider:

Mount Sinai
The Mount of Beatitudes

Mount Sinai is the place where Moses received God's Law (see Exodus 31). The Mount of Beatitudes is the Galilean hillside where Jesus famously delivered the Sermon on the Mount (see Matthew 5). For many, these two famous mountains emotionally represent the two testaments. Here are the images that most readily come to mind: On Mount Sinai stands Moses, holding the stone tablets on which are written God's Law. On the Mount of the Beatitudes sits Jesus, holding children on his knee. The tone of voice in the first scene is stern: "Thou shalt not." The second voice, however, is gentle and compassionate: "Come unto me."

When you and I picture Mount Sinai, the scene is probably foreboding and volcanic. There is thunder and lightning, thick smoke, and a loud trumpet. The mountain stands in the midst of the wilderness. It is rugged, arid, and ominous. The slopes of the mountain are forbidden, cordoned off. The people shrink back in fear.

When we picture the Galilean hillsides where Jesus taught, however, the scene is vastly different. The sky is blue and the grass is green. The slopes are gentle and fertile rather than rugged and dry. Birds of the air and lilies of the field are nearby, where Jesus can reference them and the crowds can see them. The space is not foreboding but inviting. The people do not cower and stand back from God; they eagerly gather around and press close to Jesus.

Sinai and Galilee. These are the pictures that tend to capture our prevailing associations with the Old and New Testaments. One harsh and the other friendly. One judgmental and the other inviting. Is it any wonder that most of us are much more attracted to the one and far less comfortable with the other?

What I've Heard

By their very nature, rumors are almost always imprecise, if not wildly inaccurate. As the word gets passed from one person to another, it picks up layers of individual insight and personal prejudice. And because rumors often have a loose relationship to facts, there is a lot of room for interpretation. As such, what I've heard of this rumor, in different places at different times, has varied. But there are some common themes.

The recurring central theme is that God seems different in the New Testament than God seems in the Old Testament. In the Old Testament, the Lord appears to be more angry and destructive. There is a lot of judgment and death. God seems impatient and exclusive.

In the New Testament, by contrast, the Lord appears to be kind and gracious, merciful and forgiving. God's basic posture is inviting, and the invitation is open to all.

Our natural preference, of course, is for the New Testament's portrayal of God, and so we assume that it is a more accurate representation. And that, in turn, leads to a conclusion that the Old Testament is in some way inferior. Either the Old Testament is inferior to the New Testament because it offers a less accurate portrait of God, or it is inferior because it is outdated, divinely replaced by a "new and improved" approach that is revealed and represented by the New Testament. That discounted view of the Old

Testament, then, often results in a kind of dismissal of the first two-thirds of the Bible. Because we feel the Old is either inaccurate, outdated, or both, we are free to set it aside. And, either consciously or practically, we function as though there is nothing for us to learn from the Old Testament.

But what if this rumor is incorrect? What if God is not actually different in the Old Testament than he is in the New? If the rumor is wrong—and I most certainly believe it is wrong—then we need to go back and set up all of the dominoes that were knocked over by the initial misunderstanding.

I'm very concerned about this rumor. Why? Because it is a damaging business anytime we hear and believe something about another person that is not true, and it is profoundly damaging when it is about God. The problem is not merely that some people "out there" are saying these things about God, but that we—the church—have thought or perpetuated this rumor ourselves. This is serious business because it is both theological, involving what we believe about God and the Bible, and personal, impacting our faith, our relationship with God, and our daily living. Our relationships with God and the Bible affect our relationships with the community of faith. Each one enhances the other, and each is a process that moves from introduction to acquaintance to familiarity to intimacy and love.

Over the years, as I have tried to introduce folks to the Bible and help them grow, I have encountered this rumor countless times. People come across passages that trouble or confuse them, and they come away from the Bible with the suspicion that God is different in the New Testament than in the Old.

Our endeavor in this book, therefore, is to see the two testaments more clearly so that we have an accurate picture of God. We can't walk through every chapter of the Bible in these pages, but we can walk through certain principles and themes that will help us read the whole Bible with a clearer vision and a better understanding. When we're done, we will be better acquainted with the unity of Scripture and better equipped to wrestle with difficult passages in a framework that encompasses the Old and New Testaments alike. And, in the process, we will rediscover the one who is the God of the whole Bible.

2

Nothing New
Under the Sun

Gaining Some Historical Perspective

The rumor going around the church is going around outside the church as well. The impression that God is different in the Old and New Testaments is prevalent among the general public, and although the conversation is not as informed as in the church, we see the paradigm even in popular culture.

Consider an episode from the NBC television drama *The West Wing*. President Josiah Bartlet, the central character of the show, talks with Senator Arnold Vinick about matters of personal faith. They begin by wondering together whether a candidate's religious convictions should be important to the public, but then the conversation turns to Senator Vinick's own personal journey. Vinick shares that he used to be more religious, but as he began to read the Bible more seriously, he was increasingly troubled by what he found there. He laments the use of the death penalty for matters like working on the Sabbath and committing adultery. President Bartlet smiles knowingly and interjects sympathetically, "I'm more of a New Testament man myself."[1]

Do you hear the rumor buried within President Bartlet's statement, unquestioned and unchallenged? The words of this fictional president illustrate a common sentiment: people often prefer the New Testament over the Old Testament and, without even realizing it, we may choose between them as well, aligning ourselves with one over the other.

Preference for the New Testament is not only very prevalent but also very old. In fact, as we'll discover, the common complaints about the Old Testament are not really a modern problem at all.

Not a Modern Problem

Nineteen hundred years ago, a man named Marcion was one of the first vocal critics of the Old Testament. As the wealthy son of a Christian bishop from Asia Minor, Marcion began life in orthodox Christianity. Yet as he grew and read the Bible, he came to feel that the God portrayed in the Old

Testament is arbitrary and vindictive while the God revealed as the Father of Jesus Christ in the New Testament is loving and compassionate. His sense was that the Old Testament God demands to be obeyed while the Father of Jesus desires only to be loved.

I have met a lot of church folks who would agree with Marcion's observation. The question, then, is what are we to do when we encounter problematic passages or patterns in Scripture?

Marcion's response was dramatic. He concluded that the God of the Old Testament was actually a different God than the Father of Jesus Christ. In his judgment, there was a complete separation between the two testaments, and so there was no sense in which the Old Testament was Christian Scripture. Consequently, he taught that the Old Testament was to be dismissed entirely by Christians and that our faith needs to be based only on certain epistles of Paul and Marcion's own revision of the Gospel of Luke. In fact, Marcion is known in church history for creating his own version of the Bible.

In a sense, Marcion did boldly what many other Christians do covertly, or even subconsciously. Many believers have fashioned a kind of Bible of their own: the portions they read, the parts they follow. Though they would not have the courage to take scissors to the Bible, they do it in practice and without apology.

While I think that Marcion was entirely wrong, I give him credit for being intellectually honest. He carried his beliefs through to their natural conclusions. But while he was intellectually honest, he was not intellectually rigorous, because he only identified a problem; he did not solve it. Eventually, Marcion was rejected as a heretic and thrown out of the church in Rome because of his unorthodox views and teachings, but he went on to form a church of his own. In time, Marcionism became a movement, which lasted for several centuries.

This rumor about God, you see, has been going around the church for a very long time. I expect that most Christians today have never heard of Marcion and his movement. The earliest centuries of church history generally receive scant attention in most of our congregations, and so we are unaware of the doctrinal struggles that helped the ancient church define orthodoxy and forge its creeds. As a result, many Christians may actually be closet Marcionites without knowing it.

Two Dilemmas

Return with me to *The West Wing* episode I mentioned earlier. After President Bartlet told Senator Vinick that he was "more of a New Testament man," the two exchanged comments that prompted the senator to admit, "Let's just say I struggled for a long time with that book and then finally, I just gave up the struggle."[2] These two characters express two common responses to the same dilemma. Though they are only fictional politicians, they represent very real constituencies.

For the folks in Bartlet's jurisdiction, the challenge is an intellectual one. They struggle to harmonize the two testaments, and so they pit them against each other, as though they are in opposition. Vinick, meanwhile, represents folks for whom the challenge is or becomes a spiritual crisis. These souls are so troubled by what they read that they set aside the Bible and perhaps faith altogether. Let's consider both camps.

An Intellectual Challenge

Bartlet is a natural heir to Marcion. He does not go so far as Marcion, yet his conclusions undermine either the unity of Scripture or the character of God. And those are fundamental, doctrinal issues of the Christian faith.

I am reminded of trying to solve a Sudoku puzzle. The puzzle is a nine-by-nine grid, which is divided into nine three-by-three grids. When you start the puzzle, a few spaces in the grid have been filled in for you with single digits, from 1 through 9. The challenge is to fill in the remaining spaces correctly so that each column will utilize all nine digits once; each row will use all nine digits once; and each three-by-three grid will use all nine digits once.

If a person were to focus on only filling out one three-by-three grid, the task would be easy. It wouldn't be hard to fill in a three-by-three grid so that each number was used only once. But if you were to look down the column and across the row at the other grids you would inevitably find some conflicts there. The puzzle as a whole wouldn't come together.

Similarly, President Bartlet's statement works well within the confines of one grid. That is to say, he has chosen for himself how he likes to read the Bible. And if he doesn't look beyond himself and his own sensibilities, he'll be fine. But when we look down the column, so to speak, we discover a conflict with these two fundamental, orthodox Christian doctrines. What works for him personally creates serious problems elsewhere.

First is the doctrine that God is unchanging. Near the end of the Old Testament, God says: "I the LORD do not change" (Malachi 3:6). It is a reflection of the perfection and purity of God's character. And philosophically we wonder whether it is even possible for one who is eternal to change over time. To prefer God in the New Testament over the Old, therefore, is to come in conflict with the constancy of God's nature.

Second is the doctrine of the reliability of Scripture. If we grant that God is unchanging but insist that God seems to change from the one testament to the other, then the fault must lie in the written record. And if the written record is unreliable, then we face a larger problem when it comes to our understanding of God.

Bartlet's intellectual preference for the New Testament does not solve the puzzle satisfactorily. He has narrowly pleased his own sensibilities, but he has done so at the expense of doctrine. And he is not alone. Because many others struggle with this same dilemma, we will explore both the reliability of Scripture and the reliability of God in later chapters.

A Spiritual Challenge

While President Bartlet's dilemma is intellectual, Senator Vinick's struggle is spiritual. His statement reflects a faith crisis that has become terminal: "Finally, I just gave up the struggle." That's cry-of-the-heart stuff, and the pastor in me wants to respond to that cry. I know better than to try to keep people from their struggles, because many of our struggles are inevitable, and perhaps even necessary. But giving up the struggle altogether is tragic. Because deep inside we long to believe, and the Lord wants us to believe too. But there are so many obstacles to belief.

We need to see those obstacles in a larger context. It's easy to think our struggles are unique to us as individuals. That view isolates us, though, and may make us punish ourselves or wonder what's wrong with us when we doubt. It's also easy to think that our struggles are unique to our generation, to our time and place, but that leads to an arrogance that separates us from the wisdom of those who have gone before us.

We see in the ancient pages of Scripture how common and how old are the obstacles to belief. Job struggled when his tragic experiences seemed incongruous with the character of God. The spies who investigated the Promised Land had a hard time believing God when God told them they would easily conquer a land filled with formidable foes (Numbers 13–14). Eve failed to have confidence in God's love when she heard a misleading voice telling her otherwise (Genesis 3). The disciples in the storm found it difficult to believe when they were frightened (Mark 4:35-41). And the father who asked Jesus to heal his child recognized within himself a mixture of both belief and unbelief that Jesus could actually heal him (Mark 9:14-29), which is probably a fair description of most of us.

The fictional Senator Vinick struggled to reconcile what he wanted to believe about God with what he read in Scripture, and so he gave up the struggle. The struggle is necessary. Giving up is not. As we work through this struggle together, we will discover beautiful truths about God and God's Word.

3

The Write-In Candidate

Affirming the Unity of Scripture

Imagine that it is an election year. The primaries are over, and each party has nominated its presidential candidate. Each presidential candidate has, in turn, selected his or her running mate for the office of vice president. The pair—president and vice president—are a two-for-one package. They will be elected—or not elected—together.

But what if you, as a voter, are more enthusiastic about one of the vice presidential candidates than you are about any of the presidential candidates? Will it do any good to write-in that vice presidential candidate's name on your ballot for president? Not likely, because the vice presidential candidate is only there to support the presidential candidate. In fact, you'll actually be voting against the person you really want in office!

Let us attach some names to illustrate the point. The presidential candidate is Moses, and his running mate is Matthew. If I like Matthew better than Moses, I might try to cast my vote for Matthew for president, but the irony is that Matthew himself voted for Moses. And so, even though I say I am on Matthew's side, I am not, for Matthew is on Moses' side!

When we say that we prefer the New Testament over the Old, it's as if we are sidling up to Matthew instead of Moses. But Matthew has already endorsed Moses. In effect, we are taking a position of which the writers of the New Testament themselves would not approve. Just as you cannot endorse a vice presidential candidate without endorsing the presidential candidate, you cannot favor the New Testament without favoring the Old. Let's unpack that together.

The Gospel According to Moses

Throughout the Gospels—and all of the New Testament— we see the fulfillment of what has already been recorded in the Old Testament. For example, Luke reports in his Gospel that on Easter Sunday afternoon, two of Jesus' followers were walking along the road to Emmaus, a small village just about seven miles from Jerusalem. We don't know what the purpose of their trip to Emmaus was, but whatever it was, it was eclipsed by the unexpected thing that happened to them on the way there.

Suddenly, the two men had a traveling companion. In a largely pedestrian culture, perhaps it was not surprising for one traveler to engage in conversation with another traveler on the same road. What these confused and grieving disciples did not realize, however, was that the fellow traveler was Jesus. That recognition did not happen until he broke bread with them at their dinner table in Emmaus.

While they walked and talked together, Jesus asked the men questions, which prompted them to tell him about the very eventful past few days. Jesus listened patiently as they told him things he already knew. Then he began to tell them the things they needed to know: "Beginning with Moses and with all the prophets, He explained to them the things concerning Himself in all the Scriptures" (Luke 24:27 NASB).

The immediate implication of the passage in context is that the disciples should not have been surprised by the recent events they witnessed because all those things had been foretold and foreshadowed. They were necessary, and they were predicted years before.

Beyond what Jesus was saying about recent events, he also was making a dramatic claim about the Old Testament. The phrase "the law and the prophets" is a shorthand way of referring to the Jewish scriptures—what we know as the Old Testament (see, for example, Matthew 7:12 and Acts 13:15). So when Luke says that Jesus explained what was written about him "beginning with Moses and with all the prophets," that is a reference to the Old Testament. Even though Jesus did not appear on the scene until several centuries after the last Old Testament book was written, he claimed that elements in those ancient books were written about him.

This is a remarkable claim, though it may be so familiar to us that we take it for granted. While our significance and impact are limited to the present and future, Jesus was claiming a significance so profound that it reaches back into the past—ancient books told about him *in advance* of his coming.

The Old Testament teaching that Jesus shared with those two disciples on Easter afternoon was echoed with the larger group later that evening. The two had hurried back from Emmaus to Jerusalem. And while they were with the other disciples, reporting what they had just experienced, suddenly Jesus appeared in their midst. He reassured them, proved his identity, and then declared, "All things which are written about Me in the Law of Moses and the Prophets and the Psalms must be fulfilled" (Luke 24:44 NASB). And then, "He opened their minds to understand the Scriptures" (v. 45 NASB).

Both that afternoon and evening, Jesus taught a kind of Bible study to his disciples. We don't have the content of what he said, but we know the general theme. He was claiming that much was written about him in the Old Testament, and evidently he elaborated on that material for the sake of his followers.

While we don't have a transcript of what Jesus taught that day, other passages in the New Testament might give us a clue. The writer of the Letter to the Hebrews, for example, points out the presence of Christ in much of the levitical code of the Old Testament Law—in the Tabernacle and priesthood, the sacrifices and holidays, and the blood. The Gospel writers, meanwhile, point back to specific passages from the Old Testament and identify these laws as fulfilled by Jesus. And the apostles, too, based their preaching on Old Testament texts.

This preaching and teaching from the Old Testament reminds me of a time during my first year of college, when I was asked to preach every other week at a little country church outside of town. That church shared a pastor with three other small, rural churches in the area, so twice a month they had me fill in. I didn't have a car of my own, so the pastor would drive into town on Saturday afternoons and pick me up to stay the night in his guest room. Most of those Saturday evenings together, we would talk about what each of us was planning to preach the next morning. After several months of this pattern, he remarked, "You seem to preach a lot from the Old Testament. I almost always preach from the New." It wasn't a criticism or a challenge; just an observation.

I have thought often about his observation through the years. Now, with a much larger frame of reference, I would concur that I probably do preach from the Old Testament more than many of my colleagues. But I am in excellent company, for I preach from the same texts as the apostles did.

The Book of Acts does us a great favor by recording some samples of the preaching that characterized the early church. We hear Peter preach on Pentecost (chapter 2) and in the Temple following a healing (chapter 3). We read Stephen's lengthy proclamation on the day he was martyred (chapter 7). We are privy to Peter's message to Cornelius's household (chapter 10). And we have records of what Paul preached in Pisidian Antioch (chapter 13) and Athens (chapter 17). In addition to these early "sermons," we also have an account of Paul's message to the crowds when he was arrested in the Temple (chapter 22) and his defenses before the Jewish Council (chapter 23) and Agrippa (chapter 26).

Taken all together, we observe a striking pattern. When the New Testament disciples preached, they preached from the Old Testament. That's not to say that they bypassed the events of Jesus' earthly life and ministry; not at all. But they proclaimed those events against the backdrop of Old Testament passages, which give them both authority and meaning.

In addition to samples of preaching in the early church, Acts also includes narrative summaries. We read, for example, that Apollos was effective at "proving from the Scriptures that Jesus was the Messiah" (Acts 18:28 NIV). Paul had a similar ministry in Thessalonica (Acts 17:1-3). And, shortly after, we see that the commendable souls in Berea "examined the Scriptures every day to see if what Paul said was true" (17:11 NIV). What were these scriptures they were proving and examining? The Hebrew Scriptures—or the texts of the Old Testament! You see, those texts were not set aside in favor of Jesus; instead they were the very texts used to reveal Jesus.

It is not surprising that the Hebrew Scriptures were authoritative for the Jews, but those same Scriptures continued to be authoritative in the early church as well. Moses and the prophets were not overthrown by the coming of Jesus, nor was the Old Testament replaced by the apostles' proclamation of Christ. Instead, their proclamation of Christ was rooted in the Old Testament. They saw themselves joining Moses and the prophets in bearing witness to Christ.

When Paul wrote to his spiritual son, Timothy, he affirmed Timothy's heritage of faith. He recalled the faith of Timothy's mother and grandmother, recognizing that "from infancy you have known the Holy Scriptures" (2 Timothy 3:15 NIV). That is a reference to the books of the Old Testament. Paul goes on to say in that verse that those Scriptures "are able to make you wise for salvation through faith in Christ Jesus."

Far from being antithetical to Jesus, the Old Testament actually leads us to faith in him.

Paul's Argument

We see this principle of the New Testament affirming the Old Testament in the writings of the Apostle Paul, including in his letter to the Galatians. The Christians in Galatia needed a course correction. They had been evangelized by Paul, but since that time they had fallen under the influence of some other leaders, whose influence detoured the Galatians' faith. Those other influencers are sometimes referred to as the Judaizers—Jewish Christians who believed, in effect, that a person had to become Jewish in order to be a Christian.

Jesus was Jewish, all of his disciples were Jewish, and the earliest Christians were all Jewish; so when Gentiles started to come to faith in Christ, it posed a genuine theological dilemma for the early church: Does Christ offer a direct flight to a right relationship with God, or does one have to catch a connecting flight through the Law of Moses?

The Judaizers had persuaded the believers in Galatia that compliance with the Mosaic Law was essential. And circumcision, the physical sign of the old covenant, was a special point of emphasis for them. Circumcision, the Galatians were told, was necessary for a right relationship with God. But the Apostle Paul was vigorous in his objection to the Judaizers. This was not an innocent disagreement, in his judgment. There was no agree-to-disagree on this issue, for Paul regarded the teaching of the Judaizers as fundamentally undermining the gospel of Christ. Now we might think that

Paul was dismissing the Old Testament law as obsolete, that it has been replaced by Christ; but in truth, Paul was doing a much more sophisticated thing than replacing old with new. He denied the notion that he was teaching something new at all, for the gospel he preached was an affirmation of what was old.

The doctrine that emerged in Paul's corrective letter to the Galatians is justification by faith. He wanted those believers to understand how we are made right with God— not by circumcision or straining to fulfill the demands of the Law. Rather, we are put right with God through Christ, and we access that righteousness by faith.

In Paul's understanding, this was not a "new" doctrine or a new way of God doing business with human beings. Instead, he argued that this has always been the nature of God's dealing with us. Faith has always been the way by which we are made right with God. Paul pointed back to an episode from Abraham's life recorded in Genesis 15. The Lord made a promise to Abraham on that occasion— an improbable promise, that the elderly, childless Abraham would have numerous descendants—and the narrator reports that Abraham "believed the LORD; and the LORD reckoned it to him as righteousness" (Genesis 15:6). Paul noted this moment in both his letter to the Galatians (3:6) and his letter to the Romans (4:3). Since this particular episode from Abraham's life predated God's instruction to circumcise (Genesis 17:10-27), Paul reasoned that Abraham was made righteous by God apart from both circumcision and the Law (Galatians 3:6). How? By faith. He believed God, you see, and the Lord credited that to him as righteousness.

Paul bolstered his case further by citing a revelatory moment from the prophet Habakkuk: "It is evident that no one is justified before God by the law," Paul insisted, because "the one who is righteous will live by faith" (Galatians 3:11, citing Habakkuk 2:4). Later the apostle further buttressed his argument with an illustration from the Old Testament story of Sarah, Hagar, and their sons (Galatians 4:21-31).

Paul's line of reasoning is important at so many levels, primarily because it expresses a foundational truth about the nature of our relationship with God. But, for our specific purposes here, Paul's argument also demonstrates a key principle in understanding the relationship between the Old and New Testaments.

What God offers us in Christ is new, to be sure, as well as superior to the old covenant. But it is not a departure from the old covenant. On the contrary, what God has done in Christ is an extension of what he had done before. And so it is that both Abraham and we are justified by faith. There is continuity in the plan and the pleasure of God. That is as it should be, of course, for the nature of God is unchanging.

A Book About Jesus

If I asked the average Sunday school class to identify which books of the Bible are written about Jesus, the standard response would probably be, "Matthew, Mark, Luke, and John." And that would be the right answer—well, almost.

On the first night of a class I was teaching on the Book of Revelation, I handed out a questionnaire that included this question: "What would most folks say that the Book of Revelation is about?" The unanimous answer—"the end times"—was what I had expected. But the title I had given to that short-term study was *Jesus Revealed*. Why? Because my contention was that, more than any events past, present, or future, and more than any human character from the pages of history or on the world's stage today, the most important thing revealed in Revelation is Jesus himself. And so, over the course of those weeks together, I challenged the class members to rethink the Book of Revelation and consider it instead a book about Jesus.

I recently learned that in American Sign Language the sign for Bible is the sign for Jesus combined with the sign for "book." So, in sign language, Bible is literally defined as "Jesus book." I embrace that definition because it's true!

The entire Bible, including the Old Testament, is about Jesus. As we've seen from the writers of the New Testament, who often reference the writing of Moses, the psalms of David, and the preaching of the prophets, even the books of the Bible that were written *before* Jesus' incarnation were about him. The God of the old covenant who offered justification by faith is the same God of the new covenant who offers salvation through faith in Jesus Christ. The consistency and unchanging nature of God's Word stands.

4

Out on a Limb
with a Saw

Affirming the Reliability of Scripture

I have been part of seven tours to the Holy Land, and I've experienced seven different guides there. On my most recent trip, our guide was a Palestinian Christian from Bethlehem. He was an excellent teacher.

When our itinerary took us to Jericho, the tour group gathered at one of the excavation sites, ready to hear what our guide would teach us. The story of Joshua and the battle of Jericho is one of the most familiar in Scripture. And so I sensed in our group a particular eagerness, for they felt that they began with a base of knowledge on which they could build.

Our guide was not so effusive at this site. He covered unenthusiastically some historical and archaeological details, but he did not elaborate on the biblical story there as he did in most other places. Instead, he observed that a story about a people who came into a land that belonged to other people, who conquered it and occupied it, all with a claim of God's blessing, was hard for him to swallow. And then he concluded, "I do not like having the story of Joshua and the battle of Jericho in the Bible."

The moment was revealing to me at several levels. It gave me a tender insight into his heart and the plight of his people. It offered a somewhat different perspective on a familiar and generally cherished Bible story. And it also articulated a refreshing honesty: he admitted that he simply didn't like that particular story being in the Bible.

Perhaps we would do well to employ such simple candor in our relationship with Scripture. We might be better off if we simply admitted what stories and teachings we don't like. If we did, then we could reflect more honestly on *why* a given passage is uncomfortable for us instead of discounting and reasoning away the passages with which we are uncomfortable. Our candid tour guide knew himself and his situation well enough to recognize his discomfort. How well do you and I recognize ours?

Recognizing Our Discomfort

My wife, Karen, controls the thermostat in our house. She is, by her own admission, much more temperature sensitive than I am, so it makes sense for her to set the temp.

I sometimes tease her, however, for equating "I feel" with "it is." Do you recognize the pattern? When she *feels* cold, she says that "it is" too cold. No one else in the house may feel that way, but still that is the assessment: "It's too cold in here!"

We may do the same sort of thing with Scripture. Each of us has our own comfort range, and so each of us is bound to come across passages that make us uncomfortable. The question, though, is how will we label that discomfort? Will we admit, "I feel," or will we instead declare, "It is"?

Our tour guide was frank about the familiar story of Jericho. He admitted that he didn't like the story. He didn't try to insist to us, however, that the story was wrong. And therein lies a crucial difference: if I don't like something in the Bible, does that automatically mean there is something wrong with the Bible?

We see this issue at the heart of the question of this book: *When Did God Become a Christian?* People come across things in the Old Testament that trouble or offend them, and the common reflex is to dismiss those passages by saying, "Well, but that's in the Old Testament." Do you see how that approach short-circuits our relationship with the Bible? Now we don't have to wrestle with a certain passage as a legitimate part of God's written Word, for we have discounted it. We have relegated it to a kind of archive folder, where we keep things that are outdated and no longer relevant. And so we resolve our discomfort, not by taking time to explore what we feel and why we are uncomfortable with the passage, but by simply declaring, "It is wrong/outdated/irrelevant."

This rationale has two problems. First, we do not go so far as to dismiss everything that is in the Old Testament, which makes our dismissiveness selective. And second, we do not embrace everything that is in the New Testament, which makes our stated rationale suspect. Yet to get rid of our discomfort, we often carelessly draw a line between the Old and New Testaments rather than identify and address why we are uncomfortable.

The Line Forms Here

The careless line that we draw between the Old and New Testaments is natural, to be sure. But if we are honest, the line does not really solve our problem at all. There are too many portions of the Old Testament that we want to affirm, and there are too many elements of the New Testament with which we are uncomfortable.

Rejecting something simply on the grounds that it is in the Old Testament is sloppy. What Jesus identifies as the two greatest commandments—loving God with all you've got and loving your neighbor as yourself—both come from the Old Testament. David's testimony that the Lord is his shepherd is found in the Old Testament. Instructions to care for the poor and the orphaned are in the Mosaic Law. Amos's call for justice, Isaiah's portrait of true worship, Hosea's proclamation of God's intimate and unchanging love for Israel, Jeremiah's promise of a new covenant and new hearts—these are all part of the Old Testament treasury. When we dismiss something because it is in the Old Testament, do we dismiss all of these as well?

The problem, you see, is not with the Old Testament as a whole. The fact is that we only take issue with certain parts of it. But then, when we turn the page and begin to read the New Testament, is our problem solved? Do we enter into a territory that is free from such conflict? No. Instead, the same scissors that cut up the Old Testament into appealing and troubling parts go to work on the New.

Throughout my years of ministry, I have heard a lot of folks speak dismissively of the Old Testament. Yet I have not observed total contentment with the New, either, which suggests that the Old was not really the problem. Many folks are uncomfortable, for example, with some of the things that Paul wrote. And so they counter those passages, saying, "But Jesus never taught that," or "Jesus never talked about that."

What then begins as a canon of sixty-six books is gradually whittled down to just the red-letter passages in four of those books. That's a very small Bible that some people unwittingly propose. And are they content? Are they at peace with what is left, with everything that Jesus says? Probably not since some of Jesus' teachings are among the most uncomfortable passages in the Bible. Whole books have been devoted to exploring the so-called "hard sayings" of Jesus.

We can attempt to draw lines in order to isolate our problems with Scripture. We can draw one between the Old and New Testaments, and we can draw another between Jesus and the rest of the New Testament. But in the end we discover that the line begins and ends with us. We cannot neatly subdivide or repackage the book to our liking, for no matter where we look, we will find some things that we do not like.

A Different Day

One Christmas season our family was watching the 1946 classic *It's a Wonderful Life*, starring Jimmy Stewart and Donna Reed. George Bailey, the character played by Stewart, is an altogether good guy. The audience likes him and sympathizes with him from the very start. But halfway through the movie, my daughters were surprised to see George Bailey smoking a cigarette in one scene. These days they are unaccustomed to seeing TV and movie characters smoking, and typically when they do see it, the character is rather sinister—not indicative of the lovable George Bailey character they had come to admire.

"Oh, that was a different day," my wife and I explained. "Cigarette smoking was different in our country back then. More people smoked, people smoked in more places, and it was viewed differently than it is today."

It was a different day. This is the other lens through which we commonly read Scripture. It is the friendly, albeit somewhat condescending, way that we try to handle the uncomfortable passages. When we find that lines are not easily drawn to dismiss just one section of the Bible, we discover that we can filter virtually anything displeasing by chalking it up to "a different day."

We see this phenomenon played out in a thousand ordinary ways. We look back with amusement at the clothes that were in fashion when we were teenagers. We joke about how big, clunky, and not "smart" our first mobile phones were. We shake our heads about the speed of our old dial-up connections. *It was a different day,* we say.

When it comes to Scripture, we tend to use phrases like *time bound* and *culture bound* to describe hard-to-swallow references. The reasoning goes like this: The Bible was written long ago and far away, and it is naturally a reflection of its time and place. In some respects, it is also reckoned to be a kind of prisoner of its time and place. Those ancient Near Eastern authors can't be blamed for what they didn't know and didn't understand then and there. Consequently, they are bound by their time and limited by their culture. We may discount or ignore some of what they wrote, therefore, because "it was a different day."

The Bubble Beneath

Early in our married life, my wife, Karen, was the queen of contact paper. She could work magic, turning ordinary or even grimy looking things into quite attractive redemptions.

And I would watch in amazement as she worked so carefully to measure, cut, apply, and smooth the contact paper in its place. The trick with contact paper, though, is that it's easy to get a crease in the paper or a bubble below the surface as you lay the paper down. And when you get a bubble, it is very hard to eliminate. You can move it around beneath the surface, but that just changes its location; you aren't really getting rid of it.

We need to consider that we may just be moving the bubble around when it comes to our problem passages in the Bible. For when we try to resolve our problem by saying this or that part of the Bible is time bound or culture bound, we find that we have shifted the problem elsewhere. By making that claim, now the passage in question is not so bothersome, but instead we have a problem with Scripture as a whole.

For example, if we chalk it up to the ancient time and place the fact that Abraham walked instead of drove a car, Scripture is not harmed. But if we discount how God is revealed because of the time, or if we are dismissive of something God said because of the culture of the people at the time, then we have created a serious problem. We may have made Scripture an unreliable basis for our faith.

The familiar song declares, "Jesus loves me, this I know, for the Bible tells me so." It's easy to underestimate those words because we think of them as kids' stuff. Yet that simple phrase speaks to the very heart of our faith, for it features the love of Christ, personal assurance, and the foundation of our beliefs. How do we know that Jesus loves us? Or, for that matter, how do we know that the Lord is like a shepherd, that God invites us to love mercy and do justly, or that God commands us to love our neighbor? We know because the Bible tells us so. But if we are selective about what the Bible tells us about God, ourselves, one another, or life in this world, then we exchange the basis of our faith—the Bible—for a foundation built only upon one of our own reason and taste.

There is a great irony in this, of course. We set ourselves up as the judge of Scripture because we reckon that it is time bound and culture bound. But what are we? Are we not also products of our time? Are we not also reflections of our culture? And if so, doesn't that make our interpretation of Scripture very small-minded? C. S. Lewis recognized such generational parochialism in his day, and he saw in it a terrible arrogance. Writing several decades before our own, he noted that "no one stands outside the historical process; and of course no one is so completely enslaved to it as those who take our own age to be, not one more period, but a final and permanent platform from which we can see all other ages objectively."[3]

Even apart from any assertion of divine inspiration, the practical reality is that the Bible is bigger, broader, and older than we are. It is the product of many authors hailing from a variety of places over a long period of time. Frankly, it is less bound than we are.

Interestingly, we know enough to see the fault in others' selective reading of the Bible. We are appalled, for example, at those unconscionable husbands through the generations whose favorite verse was "Wives, submit yourselves to your own husbands" (Ephesians 5:22 NIV), but who were evidently unacquainted with the verses that follow about husbands loving as Christ loves. We recognize in them that such a pick-and-choose reading of God's Word is self-serving and dishonest. So we must guard against any pick-and-choose approach in ourselves.

It is my hope that, as we continue this journey together, we will grow more comfortable with difficult portions and patterns in Scripture. But may comfort not come at the expense of the Bible—minimizing, equivocating, or dismissing. No, let us proceed with a hearty confidence in both God and the written Word—certain that God is *all* good, and that the Bible is too.

5

Israel's Home Movies

Getting a Clearer Picture of God

Karen and I met when we were teenagers—we caught each other's eye when we were high school students, and we have been together ever since. But we did not know one another as children. So it was my privilege some years ago to sit with her family as they watched old home movies. The footage was grainy and silent, yet still it was delightful to see my wife, her brothers, and her parents when they were all much younger. I was impressed by how familiar she seemed. Even though I hadn't known her then, I still recognized her. She was so obviously herself.

That may not seem like much of a revelation to you. After all, most of us would expect to have that sort of experience when watching the childhood footage of someone we know and love as an adult. In both appearance and temperament, we would expect our loved one to be familiar, recognizable.

If that is our expectation with a human being, how much more should that be our expectation with God? Human beings, after all, do change. Not only do we physically grow and age, but also there are things about our personalities, interests, habits, and behaviors that change over time— sometimes dramatically. For example, I have had very dark hair all of my adult years, and it surprises my children to know that I was a towhead as a boy. I am an early-to-bed, early-to-rise person now, which no one would have predicted about me as a high school or college student. And so, even if some current friend were to recognize me in my childhood home movies, it's still true that I have changed a great deal in the intervening years.

Perhaps we might think of the Old Testament as Israel's home movies. Those stories and testimonies come out of that nation's relationship with God thousands of years ago. And so when you and I read the Old Testament, we see pictures of God that come from a time before our own. The personal and pragmatic question, then, is whether we recognize God in those old pictures.

Favorite Pictures

You and I have favorite pictures of ourselves; we also cherish some favorite pictures of people we love. It might be worth holding those pictures before our mind's eye and asking what it is about those pictures that make them favorites. As a pastor, I have the privilege of seeing such cherished family pictures each time I officiate at a funeral or memorial service. At these services, the grieving family brings out the scrapbooks or creates photo boards that are put on display. All of those photos combine to form a more complete picture of the deceased, because the lone photo used in the obituary can't tell the whole story of a person's life. And so the collages are assembled—holidays and family vacations; birthday parties, anniversaries, and graduations; perhaps a goofy picture or two of the loved one laughing or dozing in a recliner.

But even then, the picture of this person's life is still incomplete. We tend to feature special events and moments in our photo boards, yet most of day-to-day life is made up of much more mundane stuff that doesn't make it into the collages. Raking leaves and washing dishes, reading books and walking dogs, paying bills and brushing teeth, changing diapers and driving to work. Add in the routine and ordinary, and the picture gets a little nearer to complete.

If all of those photos are necessary to portray a human being—finite and small—how many photos would be required to offer a complete picture of God? How many stories and testimonies would be needed to capture God's love and majesty, wisdom and compassion, justice and glory, grace and creativity, holiness and mercy—and more and more and more! So it is that we look to the Bible to tell us the complete story of God, through images both mundane and spectacular.

Of course, we will have some favorite "pictures" of God— treasured snapshots that tell us something special about the divine nature. But let us be careful how we regard the pictures that are not our favorites, because those images have something to tell us about God's nature and our response as well.

The Picture of Jesus

When pressed to identify their favorite picture of God, many Christians would probably choose a picture of Jesus. That's quite right, of course. Jesus told his disciples, "Whoever has seen me has seen the Father" (John 14:9). In a very important sense, therefore, Jesus is our picture of God.

Though many photos are required to capture the whole person, Jesus himself is sufficient to give us the whole picture of God. He did not say that the people who had seen him had caught a *glimpse* of the Father. No, if they had seen him, they had seen the Father.

Jesus offers us a complete picture of God, yet still no one image is adequate to capture all of Jesus. Accordingly, you and I probably cherish favorite snapshots of Jesus that we see in Scripture. In the sanctuary of the church I am privileged to serve these days, we have lovely stained glass windows along both side walls, as well as a large one in the front and another in the back. And all of these windows are devoted to depicting Jesus—they are all pictures of him.

What, then, is your favorite snapshot of Jesus? In your mind's eye, turn the pages with me through an abbreviated scrapbook excerpted from the Gospels. Jesus is promised by an angel and born in a manger. He is visited by shepherds and magi, and pursued by a madman king. He is baptized and tempted. He casts out demons with his words and heals the sick with his hands. He walks on water, calms storms, and feeds multitudes. He teaches about a runaway son being welcomed home by his father, and about a timid servant being cast out into the darkness by his master. He recommends turning the other cheek to a hurtful person and cutting off the hand that causes sin. He tells stories of a good Samaritan and a shrewd manager. He calls us to love no one more than him and to be perfect like the Father. His instruction is to forgive endlessly and rejoice in persecution; to become like children and not to worry about anything; to forget ourselves and to carry a cross. He is undiscriminating in his friendships, yet no-nonsense with sin and hypocrisy. He calls himself Way, Truth, Life, Light, Vine, Bread, and more. He rewards the sheep and damns the goats. He turns over tables and washes feet. He suffers quietly, dies voluntarily, and rises almost inconspicuously. And he promises to return to judge.

So which snapshot of Jesus is your favorite? Each is part of the picture of Jesus. And Jesus is the picture of God.

When God Seems Unfamiliar

Just as I recognized my wife, Karen, in old home movies filmed before I knew her, our goal should be to recognize the (perhaps unfamiliar) portraits of God painted in the Old Testament.

Now let me concede the imperfection of the analogy. I know my wife very well. But could I expect to have the same sort of experience with the home movies of someone I don't know so well? If I sit next to someone on a plane for two hours, could I be expected to pick him or her out of footage taken during childhood forty years earlier?

Of course not! After all, how often have we failed to recognize people after almost no meaningful passage of time at all? For example, if you see someone you know vaguely from work or school or church while strolling down the aisle of a grocery store or walking through the mall one day, you might freeze and think, *Who is that? I know him from somewhere. But where? What's his name? I hope he doesn't see me and call me by name!* It's hard to recognize a person in an unfamiliar context or environment.

One Saturday afternoon I stopped by the church where I was serving as pastor in order to pick up something from my office. I had been doing chores around the house that day, and so I was dressed in jeans, sneakers, a T-shirt, and a baseball cap. As I was leaving, I crossed paths with a church member in the parking lot, and it was clear that he didn't know who I was—at all. He would recognize me again the next day, of course, when I was wearing a suit, tie, and wingtips and standing at the pulpit. On that Saturday afternoon, however, I was a stranger.

The people who only hear my voice when I preach might not recognize my voice when I am cheering at a sporting event or playing with my young daughter. Have I changed? No, I just have more parts to me than that person has known to date. Likewise, when God seems unfamiliar to us in parts of the Old Testament, we should make allowances that the change may not be in God, and the fault may not be in Scripture. Perhaps it can be owed to the fact that we are unaccustomed to seeing the Lord in that particular kind of setting or role. And perhaps that means we just need to get to know God better.

Let this, then, be our deliberate goal when reading Scripture. Rather than dismissing a story because the portrait seems unfamiliar, let us take it at face value. Let us see it as an episode about the Lord from a time before we were introduced. And let us embrace that story as an opportunity to get to know God better.

Two Kinds of New

Getting to know God better requires adding to what we already know about God, which involves learning something new. And learning something new may be easy, or it may be quite hard.

Until 1930, for example, the world didn't know that Pluto existed. Then, for about seventy years, Pluto was known as the ninth planet in our solar system. More recently, astronomers have downgraded Pluto from a planet to the classification of "dwarf planet." Neither Pluto's discovery as the ninth planet or its redesignation as a dwarf planet were particularly troubling to people. In contrast, the accumulated work of Copernicus, Kepler, Galileo, and Newton created real trouble in Renaissance Europe. Traditional science and theology alike were disrupted when these men asserted that the sun, not the Earth, was at the center of our solar system. At the time, this knowledge turned everything upside down and was so dramatic and impactful that it is referred to as the Copernican Revolution.

So here are two cases of scientific discovery that changed our understanding of the universe around us. Yet one was controversial and revolutionary (the Copernican Revolution), while the other (Pluto's discovery and demotion) evokes little more than a yawn from the general population. Why the difference?

When it comes to knowledge and understanding, perhaps there are two kinds of new. You can learn something new that is *additional*, or you can learn something new that is *different*. The former is easily assimilated into current understanding, while the latter can be painfully disruptive. To add or subtract a planet from an existing model is learning something new that is merely additional. We tack it on to what we already know. But to replace an existing model with a new one is to learn something new that is different from what we have known before. And that is a much tougher learning process for most people.

It may be that the same principle applies to our understanding of God. Most of us go into our Bible reading with some knowledge—or at least an impression—about who God is and what God is like. And as we read more, we learn more. The question is whether what we learn feels merely additional or entirely different. What feels additional reinforces all that we already believe. But what feels different may be unsettling to us.

Personally, I do not want to discard anything the Bible tells me about God simply because it is different from what I already know. Rather, I want to embrace all of it. I want to come to know God better and better—even if that means having to adjust my understanding and my model in order to accommodate the whole truth. Why? Because the nature of God is at stake.

6

A God at Odds?

Clarifying the Integrity of God's Nature

I once attended a beautiful wedding that included a very thoughtful homily by the officiating minister. He began by expounding on the nature of the relationship into which the bride and groom were entering. And then, from that intimate love relationship, he transitioned naturally and rightly into the intimate love relationship that we may have with God. That prompted him to ask rhetorically, so what is the gospel message?

The minister went on to offer a survey of creation, sin, and redemption. He began by asserting the holiness of God and the perfection of God's original creation, and then he declared that because God is holy, God must punish sin. That led to a brief but vibrant description of our doom as sinners. Then the minister shifted gears from our doom to our salvation, explaining the good news of Christ's atoning death and victorious resurrection. As he moved from the first point to the second point, he said, "But God is also loving."

That statement is altogether orthodox, of course. The problem for me was one word he used: *but.*

Do you see the theology implicit in that word? The minister wasn't saying that God is holy *and* loving. Rather, he said that God is holy *but* loving. It's almost as if he was saying to the congregation, "Well, I've got good news, and I've got bad news." The love of God is the good news. But the holiness of God, it seems, is bad news for us.

Could that possibly be true? Is it possible that holiness is an undesirable attribute of God?

Two Great Attributes

Theologian Paul Jewett notes that most theologians "agree that holiness and love together describe the nature of God."[4] So the minister at that wedding was operating with a traditional paradigm. By affirming the holiness of God and the love of God above all, he was echoing the conclusion of saints and students through the ages.

Unfortunately, the preacher's "but" has also been the assumption of many folks over the years. The assumption is we know that love and holiness go together in God, but we suspect that they do not go together naturally. Instead, the all-too-common supposition is that there are two competing impulses within God—on the one hand to destroy us and on the other hand to save us. Taken as separate claims, each one can be explained, and if we could keep them separate, we might not have a problem. But, of course, they cannot be kept apart.

On the one hand, we might ask, "Why would God forgive and save a person?" And the happy answer comes back, "Because God loves us, of course!" After all, the Scriptures tell us, "For God so loved the world that he gave his only Son, so that everyone who believes in him may not perish but may have eternal life" (John 3:16).

Meanwhile, we might ask, "Why would God destroy or damn a person?" And there, too, the answer is equally straightforward. "Human beings are sinful, but God is holy. God's holiness is beyond our comprehension, and our sin is intolerable to that holiness." As Jonathan Edwards famously preached, "He is of purer eyes than to bear to have you in his sight."[5]

By itself, each statement is logical—not equally appealing, of course, but equally defensible. When we take the two statements together, however, we end up with a God who is self-contradictory. God's holiness and God's love, we conclude, are in a constant struggle over what to do with us. And that, in turn, puts us in a very precarious position. Our souls are either the beneficiary or the casualty of this divine tug-of-war. God's holiness pushes us toward hell, while God's love pulls us toward heaven. What will become of us? And if we are saved, does the holiness of God sulk in defeat?

This view of the nature of God affects how we read and interpret the two testaments. We paint with a broad brush and surmise that holiness is the primary attribute of God at work in the Old Testament. Consequently, God is quick-tempered and judgmental. We see an angry God, who is eager to wipe out whomever and whatever displeases. Love, meanwhile, is the attribute of God that we associate most with the New Testament. We picture Jesus eating with sinners and welcoming children. We see him rescuing the adulterous woman and inviting himself into Zacchaeus's life. Everyone is embraced. Everything is forgiven.

In the next several chapters, we will give closer consideration to this broad characterization of the two testaments. For now, let's consider this question: *Are the holiness of God and the love of God actually in competition with each another?*

Cleaning House

I remember as a boy hearing my mother mutter, "I can't stand a mess." Cleanliness mattered to my mom. She vacuumed and dusted thoroughly. She made sure that our dishes and silverware were impeccably clean. She liked her car to be clean on the inside and out, and my sister and I grew up with an expectation that we would keep our own rooms and spaces clean.

My mom was the type who didn't vacuum around furniture. She didn't even push the vacuum wand under it. Most of the time, she would move the furniture in order to vacuum a room as completely as possible. And so I remember well hearing her mutter, "I can't stand a mess." The noteworthy detail, though, is what she was doing when she said it. You can probably guess—she was cleaning.

A coat draped over a chair, dirty laundry left on a bedroom floor, careless fingerprints on a window, papers lying around on countertops, unwashed dishes left in the sink—these were the things she'd be dealing with. And as she remedied each situation, we might hear her muttering about the mess. But notice that it was not an empty lament; it was always accompanied by action. And the action was, we might say, redemptive. That is, she would take a setting that was messy and make it lovely again.

This, then, is the good news about God. And the good news is not exclusively an enterprise of God's love—it is also great, good news about God's holiness.

We are right to affirm that God is holy. In the next chapter, we will strive for a fuller appreciation of that holiness. But let us not fall prey to the misapprehension that God's holiness is an angry and destructive attribute. The fact that my mother couldn't stand a mess didn't lead her to blow up a messy room. No, she would clean it. In his holiness, God sets out to get rid of sin. And as we will see more clearly in the pages to come, God does not tolerate sin. But getting rid of sin does not mean getting rid of sinners. The rooms of our minds, hearts, and lives are messy, to be sure, and the Holy One wants them to be clean. And so God's endeavor is to clean them, not destroy them. Our part is to be sure that we do not cling to anything that the Holy One wants to throw away!

No "Buts" About It

The minister at the wedding was right to tell the congregation that God is holy, and he was right to preach that God is loving. His error was just one word: *but*. There is no conflict in the character of God. There is no "but." In order to appreciate that truth, we must recognize that God is significantly different from us in that we *do* have conflicts within us.

How often have you been of two minds about something? The Apostle Paul wrote, "I do not do what I want, but I do the very thing I hate" (Romans 7:15). Like Paul, so often I have said, "Part of me wants to do this, but another part of me wants to do that." It is not at all uncommon to find a "but" in me—in my will or in my behavior. My actions are inconsistent, you see, because my will is divided. And my will is divided because my character is imperfect.

To illustrate the point, imagine a woman who would say that she is "an honest woman." And in most of her words and actions, she is. She would never lie on the witness stand, for example, or forge a signature, or enter false information on her tax forms. But could she say that she is perfectly honest? Does she, for example, ever exaggerate while telling a story? Does she offer a less embarrassing explanation for some mistake she has made? Does she misrepresent her true feelings about a person or situation? Honesty is a positive— and even a prevailing—attribute with her. Yet it is imperfect, and so she will experience a division within her will and inconsistency in her behavior.

But we may press the point further. Let us say that our hypothetical person is perfectly honest. That is only one attribute, and the issue we are contemplating is a conflict between attributes. And so we wonder if this person, who is perfectly honest, is capable of being, say, perfectly kind at the same time. Don't those attributes come into conflict with each other?

For most of us, our experience is that honesty and kindness can butt heads. But that may be because we have a shallow definition of kindness. If the highest form of kindness is to prevent someone's feelings from getting hurt, then kindness will be hard to achieve, and many other virtuous things will be sacrificed on that dubious altar.

The fact is that much of what we do—or don't do—under the guise of kindness may actually be a form of selfishness. In other words, we don't want to hurt someone's feelings, and so we choose *not* to be honest. In all likelihood, however, we have only bumped the problem down the road, delegating it to someone else. Some other person along the way will be honest with the person, and so we have not really spared anyone but ourselves. If our kindness were more perfect, it would not be in conflict with our honesty.

Think of it another way. We may play two, three, or many different notes on a piano at the same time, and all the notes could be in harmony together. If one key is a little flat, however, then the harmony is broken. And so, too, many attributes can all be in harmony together, if each is perfect. When one is flat, it makes the whole sound out of tune.

There is no such conflict in God. God's attributes are perfect, and so they are in perfect harmony with one another. And there is perfect unity in God's nature. God's will is an extension of God's character, and God's actions are always a function of God's will. So there is complete integrity between who God is and what God does.

It is possible to hear the harmony of God's holiness and God's love, and during the next two chapters, we will take a closer look at each of those fundamental attributes. Rather than being at odds with each other, we will see that God's love and God's holiness are natural partners together in the same divine will. And with respect to fallen humanity, that divine will is to get rid of sin. Both God's holiness and God's love want to save you. It is in both holiness and love that the Lord forgives you. And divine holiness and love alike seek to perfect you. No "buts" about it!

7

Holy, Holy, Holy

Seeing God's Holiness in the Old and New Testaments

I was still just a young boy when I attended my first NBA game with my dad. Early in the game, a man who was sitting several rows ahead of us caught my eye. He was sitting in the very front of our section, but he was facing the wrong direction. He had his back to the game, and he was facing the stands. I was bewildered. When I pointed the man out to my dad, however, he explained to me that the man was an employee of the venue, and he was there for security. His job was not to watch the game but to watch the crowd.

At first, I thought it must have been tough to have the game going on right behind his back but not be able to watch it. Then it occurred to me that he could probably still get a pretty good idea of what was going on behind him by watching us. He could detect in our faces the action that he himself could not see.

We can read the Bible with that same perspective. As we read, we are like the security personnel, and the crowd we are facing contains all the characters in Scripture. We get to see them. And while we may not see everything that they see, we learn a great deal by watching them.

We won't see God the way that Moses, Isaiah, or Ezekiel did. And we won't see Jesus in the way that Mary, Peter, or Paul did. But we learn a great deal about God from looking in the faces of those who did see him. And here is perhaps the chief thing we learn from them: God is holy.

Two Visions, Same Scene

The Old Testament prophet Isaiah had a vision of God, famously recorded for us in Isaiah 6. We recognize this event as Isaiah's "call" experience. The setting seems to have been the Temple, which was a building in Jerusalem that Isaiah would have known well. And yet, at the same time, we sense that the prophet is really getting a glimpse into the very throne room of the universe. In the vision, the Lord is not alone. Isaiah also witnesses the seraphim that surround the throne, and we discover that they are themselves creatures of splendor and awe. Yet in the presence of God they cover their faces and cry out, "Holy, Holy, Holy is the LORD of hosts" (Isaiah 6:3 NASB).

Isaiah is overwhelmed by what he sees. "Woe is me," he exclaims, "for I am ruined!" (v. 5 NASB). In the presence of the Lord, Isaiah is overcome with the sense of his own sin and unworthiness. "I am a man of unclean lips," he cries, "and I live among a people of unclean lips" (v. 5 NASB). We are not privy to what the prophet and the seraphim saw, but we learn something about the Lord when we look into the faces of those who saw God that day. We observe that they are, at once, both quieted and full of joy. These are the ingredients of reverence. And for beings both human and supernatural, reverence is the automatic response to the divine presence, for God is holy. *Holy, holy, holy!*

The episode from Isaiah is not unique. At the end of the New Testament, the Apostle John reports a vision that he has, and it, too, offers a glimpse of heaven's throne. John offers an even more detailed description of the throne and its surroundings, and he witnesses a broader assortment of worshipers around the throne. Yet the ones who are in God's presence respond just as the seraphim in Isaiah: "Day and night they do not cease to say, 'HOLY, HOLY, HOLY, *is* THE LORD GOD, THE ALMIGHTY, WHO WAS AND WHO IS AND WHO IS TO COME'" (Revelation 4:8 NASB).

This is the cry that God evokes, for this is what God is—holy.

The Mysterious Attribute

Holiness is a difficult concept for us to grasp. We say that God is holy, but when we try to ask what holy is, the answer is "God." *Holy* is a word that really belongs exclusively to God. And when we apply the word to other things, we discover that it is not being employed in its fullness, for those things are only derivatively holy. That is, they are holy because they come from God, were ordained by God, or have been dedicated to God. But God alone is truly holy.

When applied to things or places—like a sacrament or a sanctuary—we might substitute the word *sacred*. Yet we recognize that this is an inadequate synonym when applied to God. And so we grapple with words like *transcendence*, *perfection*, and *otherness*. Theologian Thomas Oden tries to capture the fullness of the word *holy*: "The moral quality that best points to God's incomparably good character, as one incomparable in power, is holiness," Oden writes. "Holiness…implies that every excellence fitting to the Supreme Being is found in God without blemish or limit. It also implies that all other moral excellences (goodness, justice, mercy, truth, and grace) are unified and made mutually harmonious in infinite degree in God."[6]

Against such a profound backdrop, we see how foolish it is to employ this magnificent word as half of an exclamation, such as "holy cow," or worse. We human beings seek out big words to try to express what we're feeling. But *holy* is too big a word for most things. It should not be bandied about as an alternative to "wow" or "I'm surprised." It belongs to God alone, and then only to those people and things with whom God chooses to share it.

The Old Testament Law endeavored to impress upon the people of Israel the holiness of their God. The commandments bore witness to the holiness of God's name. Furthermore, the people were expected to treat with special reverence the days that the Lord had designated as holy—both the weekly Sabbath and the several other holy days identified throughout each year. Likewise, the priests, places, furniture, utensils, and sacrifices employed in the worship of God were holy inasmuch as they were set aside for his service.

Even the design of the Hebrew campsite in the wilderness was an object lesson in holiness. Though not really circular, the effect of the design was concentric circles of increasing holiness. We observe that "outside the camp" was where unclean things were sent. The next layer in was the great band of the children of Israel, camped in tribes around a designated center. Nearer that center were the campsites of the priests, the particularly holy people within Israel because they were ordained for God's service. Then came the Tabernacle compound, deliberately located right in the middle of the camp. Within that holy campus was a tent, which featured, first, the Holy Place. And, finally, on the other side of the curtain in that tent, there was the Most Holy Place, or the Holy of Holies—the particular place of God's presence.

The significance of holiness was impressed upon the people of Israel by the death penalty. In our day, we think of only the most heinous crimes against humanity as deserving of death. The Mosaic Law, by contrast, identified a number of things as capital offenses that had no human victim at all, such as working on the Sabbath. The principle was that to trespass against holiness in any way was the most serious kind of offense a human being could commit.

A Kinder, Gentler Testament?

It's hard for us to comprehend today, but when we read the Old Testament, we see that both the demands and the penalties of the Law related to God's holiness were severe. Is the situation any different in the New Testament? To answer this question, let's take a look at some of the points of commonality between the testaments on this theme.

We noted earlier the holiness of God's name. It is so serious a matter that it ranks as third of the Ten Commandments (Exodus 20:7). And misuse of God's name was one of the capital offenses in the Mosaic Law (Leviticus 24:16). When we get to the New Testament, we immediately observe the same sort of priority given to the holiness of God's name. The matter is so right under our noses, however, that we may not notice it. The model prayer that Jesus taught his disciples is generally divided into seven petitions. And what is the very first of those seven petitions? "Hallowed be thy name" (Matthew 6:9 KJV). According to Jesus, praying for God's name to be properly revered as holy is meant to be the first order of business in our prayers.

When we broaden the theme to include Jesus' name, we see that the Lord's name is arguably more prominent in the New Testament than it is even in the Old. Gathering, preaching, healing, baptizing, and praying are all to be done in Jesus' name. After Jesus' death and resurrection, the antagonists in Jerusalem were concerned above all else that the disciples should no longer teach in the name of Jesus (Acts 4:18). And Paul declared that all of creation would one day bow and acknowledge Christ as Lord in response to his name (Philippians 2:9-10).

Another issue surrounding the theme of God's holiness in the Old Testament is a frightening sense of danger. In Exodus 19, Sinai—the place where God will come down and appear to Moses—is cordoned off on penalty of death. In Leviticus 10, Nadab and Abihu are consumed instantly for offering unholy fire: "Through those who are near me I will show myself holy" is the divine explanation for the dramatic punishment (Leviticus 10:3). Likewise, in 2 Samuel 6 the seemingly well-meaning Uzzah is struck down on the spot for presuming to touch the holy ark of the covenant.

But the danger associated with God's holiness is not an unpredictable business. In fact, we should understand it just from ordinary experience. We recognize that there is a natural, even unavoidable, connection between danger and power. Household chemicals, power tools, prescription medicine, high voltage wires—none of these are bad things. Indeed, each has tremendous capacity for good. But every one of them can maim or kill when mishandled. Danger is the inevitable companion of power, and so it should not surprise us that holiness is hazardous.

We may see the same sort of phenomenon at work in the New Testament church at Corinth. Evidently the Christians there were mishandling the elements of the Lord's Supper. Paul offered them sober correction about their conduct and its consequences: "All who eat and drink without discerning the body, eat and drink judgment against themselves. For this reason many of you are weak and ill, and some have died" (1 Corinthians 11:29-30).

We teach our children to be cautious about chemicals and traffic, electrical outlets and power tools. We want them to have a healthy fear of such things. For we know that childish ignorance makes them susceptible to toying carelessly with things that are powerful. Likewise, the Law of God endeavors to educate us, lest in our ignorance we trespass against holiness.

Healthy fear is an important concept for us to carry from our parenting into our reading of Scripture. When the Bible speaks about fearing God, it is not the fear that comes when dealing with someone who is erratic or hostile. Rather, it is awed reverence: the ultimate form of taking something seriously. Just as we teach our children to take seriously things that are powerful, so it is with us and God. The prophet Isaiah pulls the pieces together for us, saying, "The LORD Almighty is the one you are to regard as holy, he is the one you are to fear" (Isaiah 8:13 NIV).

We might think that such a potent reality as God's holiness would keep us sinful human beings at a great distance. We see that is the common reflex of humility and reverence, of shame and fear. Yet shrinking back from holiness is not the perfect will of God. Instead, remarkably, the Holy One invites us into holiness. For example, consider the dietary codes of the Old Testament law. They do not generally command much of our attention today, yet tucked within those ancient instructions is a glimpse into the heart of God. In exhorting the people to avoid contact with unclean animals, God said, "I am the LORD your God; sanctify yourselves therefore, and be holy, for I am holy" (Leviticus 11:44). As God's people, we are to be holy because our God is holy.

When the Lord said, "Let us make humankind in our image, according to our likeness" (Genesis 1:16), you see, God meant it. From the beginning, it was God's expressed intent that, even in our fallen state, we should be holy, for our Maker is holy. Here we meet a profound convergence of several important truths. In quality, in character, God alone is holy. Yet whatever is chosen by God or dedicated to God becomes holy—that is, it is set apart exclusively for God, like the Tabernacle or the priests. The magnificent prospect set forth in Scripture, then, is that God's perfect will for human beings is twofold: that we should be set apart for God's service, and also that we should become increasingly like God in nature and character.

This principle becomes still more emphatic in the New Testament. Consider, for example, the opening line of Paul's letter to the Ephesians: "Paul, an apostle of Christ Jesus by the will of God, to the saints who are in Ephesus and are faithful in Christ Jesus" (Ephesians 1:1). The salutation identifies both the sender and the recipients, and he gives titles to each. Paul calls himself *apostle*. And he calls the believers in Ephesus *saints*.

Saints is not a rare moniker in Paul's writings. Nor is it selectively applied just to the good folks of Ephesus. We see Paul use the term freely in his letters to the Romans, the Corinthians, the Philippians, and the Colossians, as well as his personal correspondences with Timothy and Philemon. I selected the verse from Ephesus, however, because *saints* is so plainly employed there as reference to all of the believers in a given place.

The underlying Greek word that we translate "saints" is not actually a plural noun. Rather, it is the Greek adjective for holy. Paul takes that adjective, makes it plural, and puts the definite article in front of it. Literally speaking, therefore, Paul is referring to the Christians in Ephesus as "the holies." Like them, we are "the holies"—the holy people of God.

This is the will and purpose of God for us. Just as God is the Holy One, we in turn are to be holy ones. The great British preacher of the last century, William Sangster, gave expression to this startling truth: "The breath-taking claim of the New Testament in regard to holiness is that while man is helpless and hopeless alone, by the power of the indwelling Spirit he can do more than keep the ancient code: he can reach up to the dizzy heights of holiness revealed by Jesus and scale the serene summit itself."[7]

Finally, in considering the theme of God's holiness across the two testaments, I am reminded of the Apostle Paul's reference to the Law as "our tutor" (Galatians 3:24 NASB). Because we tend to be only distantly familiar with the Law, however, we may be untutored in holiness. And, consequently, we are hobbled in our capacity to understand the good news presented in the New Testament.

At Mount Sinai, the people are kept back at a distance from the glory of the holy God (Exodus 19). In the design of the Tabernacle, and later the Temple, there is a deliberate, built-in separation between the people and God, whose presence is identified with the Holy of Holies.[8] Thus the people are tutored in holiness. Against that backdrop, then, stands the remarkable proclamation of the gospel: "Therefore, brothers and sisters, since we have confidence to enter the Most Holy Place by the blood of Jesus, by a new and living way opened for us through the curtain, that is, his body, and since we have a great priest over the house of God, let us draw near to God" (Hebrews 10:19-22 NIV).

The Holy One invites us to draw near. This was always the heart of God, of course: the Creator who held us close to

The veil is rent; in Christ alone the living way to heaven is seen; the middle wall is broken down, and all the world may enter in."[9]

8

Jesus Loves Me, This I Know

Seeing God's Love in the Old and New Testaments

Our first child came into the world ten days before her due date. Needless to say, we were caught very much by surprise when Karen went into labor that Friday night, and the next morning it felt surreal to be holding a tiny little baby girl who was my daughter.

I discovered for myself that morning that our natural instinct is to talk to babies. I think that's good and right, even though it makes no immediate sense. Moreover, we often ask babies questions, which is even less sensible. Without any forethought or planning on my part, what came naturally to me that morning was to look into my daughter's little face and ask her, "Do you know how much I love you?"

She didn't, of course. And even now, twenty-two years later, she still doesn't. I'm not sure that it is possible for children to comprehend their parents' love for them. Even when they grow up and have children of their own, they still may not fully internalize that what they feel for their children is what their parents felt for them.

Do you know how much I love you? It's a question I asked because I wanted her to know the answer, even though she couldn't possibly understand. Throughout my children's lives, I have told them and tried to show them that I love them, yet still they only have a small sense for how much I love them; they cannot comprehend it. And that, I suspect, is the nature of our relationship with God. We have heard over and over again that God loves us, but we cannot truly fathom the depth and breadth of that love.

The Essence of God

Throughout both the Old and the New Testaments, we are told of God's love for God's people. But the Scriptures not only tell us that God loves us; they tell us something even more profound about God's love.

Let's assume the role of a grammar student long enough to examine a very brief sentence written by the Apostle John:

"God is love" (1 John 4:16). It is so simple a statement that we might overlook it as sentimental. Yet it is precisely that simplicity that makes the sentence dramatic. The syntax is alarmingly plain: two nouns with the verb "to be" connecting them. That's it. Yet that seemingly vanilla declaration stands out as unique in all of Scripture, and it makes a startling affirmation about God.

When we see that same sort of construction elsewhere in Scripture, making a direct correlation between God and another noun, it is typically metaphorical language. For instance, the psalmist, most notably, speaks of the Lord throughout the Book of Psalms as being a refuge, stronghold, rock, shepherd, and king. What John is saying is different, however, for the corresponding noun (*love*) he uses is abstract rather than concrete. So John is referencing an attribute of God rather than a role of God.

Of course, there are plenty of verses in Scripture that speak of God's attributes. Dozens of times we read affirmations that the Lord is holy, good, mighty, just, jealous, compassionate, gracious, righteous, merciful, and on and on. In those cases, however, the construction is not noun-and-noun, but noun-and-adjective. If John had taken that approach, for example, he would have said that "God is loving," not "God is love."

John's simple declaration stands out from the rest of scriptural statements about God's attributes, because John employs the noun rather than the adjective. We read elsewhere that God is holy, but nowhere does it say that

God *is* holiness. We affirm that God is just, but that does not suggest that God *is* justice. And while God is almighty, the Bible does not equate God with might or power. Yet John says that God *is love*. Not just *loving* (as wonderfully true as that is), but love itself.

Love is God's quintessential attribute. In Latin, the verb "to be" is *esse*. We get our English word *essence* from it. And so, when John declares that God is love, he assures us that love is God's very essence. As Charles Wesley expressed it, "Thy nature and Thy name are love."[10] If love is God's very essence, then logic demands that love should be no small theme in Scripture. Love should not make just an occasional appearance or seem to be a late development in the story. Rather, the love of God is evidenced at all times and in everything God does in Scripture, and if love is God's quintessential attribute, then that should be our guide when reading Scripture.

We clearly see the love of God in the New Testament. Yet as we've acknowledged, many people perceive God to be more loving in the New Testament than in the Old Testament. Our endeavor in this chapter, then, is to see God's love more clearly and more fully in the Old Testament and, specifically, to recognize key areas where the continuity of God's love is shown in the New and the Old. In the end, we'll discover that these features of God's love so frequently associated with the New Testament actually are continuations of what is revealed in the Old Testament.

The Continuity of God's Desire for Us

Among our foremost associations with the teachings of Jesus is his emphasis on love. He identifies loving God as the first and the greatest of all the commandments, and follows that by saying that the second greatest commandment is to love one's neighbor as oneself (Matthew 22:37-39). And, near the climax of his earthly ministry, he gives his disciples yet another commandment to love—"A new commandment," he calls it, as he instructs them to love one another as he has loved them (John 13:34).

The commandment to love does not begin with Jesus, however. When he identifies the greatest commandment of all—love God first—he was selecting an existing commandment from the Mosaic Law (see Deuteronomy 6:5). The Old Testament, therefore, is the source of the commandment to love. Indeed, it is the Old Testament that commands both our vertical and our horizontal love—that is, both love of God and love of neighbor. When Jesus gives the "new commandment," therefore, he is building on a foundation of love that is laid in the Old Testament.

The skeptic has a retort, though: It is not the Old Testament that identifies loving God and loving neighbor as the greatest commandments. That prioritization comes from Jesus. The fact that those instructions are found in the Old Testament is not convincing proof enough that love is the emphasis in the Old Testament that it is in the New. Even a broken clock is right twice a day, after all.

In order to see how central to the Old Testament revelation of God the love commandments are, let us step back and consider a hypothetical question. If the question "Of all the commandments, which is the most important?" had been put to you rather than to Jesus, how would you have answered? We might congratulate ourselves to think that we would have chosen *love God*, but I wonder.

For many folks, the first instinct is more horizontal than vertical, and of all the people-oriented commandments, they might reckon the instruction not to kill as the weightiest. And even those who would think first of the God-oriented commandments would not necessarily chose *love God*. Perhaps, instead, we might exalt believe in God, worship God, or have no other gods above all the others.

For myself, I know what I would choose. My pragmatic instinct would be to say that the most important commandment is to obey God. That, after all, would encompass everything else, wouldn't it? If you obey God, then all of the other commandments would be covered automatically.

Yet "obey" was not Jesus' answer. And, as you might expect, Jesus' answer is more right than mine. For it turns out that obedience does not encompass everything else, but love does.

Jesus told his disciples, "If you love me, you will keep my commandments" (John 14:15). Obedience follows love. We gather, however, that love does not automatically follow obedience. Consider the Pharisees. They were famously particular about obeying God, yet we do not have the impression that they enjoyed a warm, love relationship with God. So what Jesus is saying is that we cannot love God without also obeying God. Untold scores of unhappy legalists, on the other hand, have managed to obey God without loving God.

And so I arrive at a conclusion that sounds almost scandalous: namely, that love is more important to God than obedience. That's not to say obedience is unimportant; rather, it is to affirm that love is primary—it comes first.

The primary importance of love is implicit from the very beginning of the biblical story. The Genesis account of Creation paints a perfect picture, but that perfection has a built-in vulnerability. It is, in some respect, fragile, for it depends upon the cooperation of the human creature. God made humankind free, and by doing so, the Lord made the beauty and harmony that characterized Eden contingent upon Adam and Eve's obedience. And we observe in the story that, when they disobeyed, something was profoundly ruined; and the story begins to deteriorate from that point forward.

With so much riding on human obedience, therefore, one might think that God would have made a greater effort to guarantee it. We know the precautions that we all take with our things we are most eager to protect. Yet the Creator seems reckless with his own creation by entrusting it all to so uncertain a custodian as human obedience.

What choice did God have? Well, the Creator could have designed human beings to be as constrained by moral laws as we are by physical laws. When we invent or design some sort of machine, we try to make it function as reliably as possible. And, if we were capable of it, we would design the thing so that it would never fail. Certainly the omniscient inventor was capable of such foolproof design.

So unless we are willing to charge God with either a design flaw or a terrible recklessness, there must have been some reason why God made things—and specifically a good reason to make us—the way that God did. We wonder why the harmony of creation was not protected better. But perhaps God was protecting something else instead—freedom.

God's risky design was protecting human freedom. And so, by extension, the design was to protect love. For if we human beings were constrained to obey, then we would not be free. And if we were not free, we could not love. And love, as I've suggested, is more important to God than obedience: not because obedience is unimportant, but because love is primary.

Love is God's nature. Naturally, therefore, it is the primary desire of God's heart. And it has been from our very beginning.

The Continuity of God's Invitation to Us

The New Testament has a great advantage over the Old that is not to be underestimated—through Jesus, we get to see God in the flesh. As Jesus told his disciples, "Whoever has seen me has seen the Father" (John 14:9).

We cherish what we see of God in Jesus. We see him gladly eating with sinners, unhesitatingly touching lepers, freeing people from all sorts of maladies, and welcoming the children the disciples had tried to shoo away. We hear him say, "Come to me, all you that are weary and are carrying heavy burdens, and I will give you rest" (Matthew 11:28), and we rejoice at the warmth of his loving invitation.

We don't see portraits of Jesus with his arms crossed, looking closed off. Instead, his posture is always open, and his demeanor is always welcoming. He proclaims that he stands at the door and knocks (Revelation 3:20), and he promises that he will not turn away anyone who comes to him (John 6:37).

In Jesus we find acceptance and forgiveness, and this we recognize as the gospel. I remember a small poster that a Christian friend of mine had inside his junior high locker. It was a picture of Jesus on the cross. And the caption read, "I asked Jesus how much he loved me, and he said, 'This much,' and stretched out his arms and died." So it is that the New Testament pulses with the loving welcome of Jesus.

The fact that God is more visible in the New Testament than in the Old, however, does not change his nature. For example, as a boy, I lived many miles from my grandparents, and so I would go many months without seeing them. I could talk to them on the phone, of course, but that experience was inferior to the experience of going to visit them and actually being with them. Yet, whether on the phone or in person, they were still the same. The experience was different, but the people were not. So it is that God's gracious invitation, welcome, and loving embrace are as real in the Old Testament as in the New Testament.

An amusing witness to this grace is the comedic prophet Jonah. He does not mean to be a comedian, but we cannot help but be entertained by his petulance and frustrations. Among other things, we observe that God is more eager to forgive than Jonah is. Jonah was perfectly happy with the prospect of the wicked city of Nineveh being destroyed as divine judgment. But when the people of Nineveh repented, the Lord withdrew judgment, and Jonah was unhappy about it. "I knew that you are a gracious God and merciful," Jonah complained, "slow to anger, and abounding in steadfast love, and ready to relent from punishing" (Jonah 4:2). In any other mouth, those words would be a testimony, a hymn of praise, but Jonah speaks them in accusation.

Once we get past Jonah's prejudices and idiosyncrasies, we see the profound beauty in his statements about God. The prophet Joel proclaimed the same truth about God's nature while expressing God's open-arms invitation:

> *Return to the* LORD, *your God,*
>   *for he is gracious and merciful,*
> *slow to anger, and abounding in steadfast love,*
>   *and relents from punishing.*
>
> *(Joel 2:13)*

The prophet Ezekiel, likewise, gives voice to the God who does not want to punish: "I have no pleasure in the death of the wicked, but that the wicked turn from their ways and live." And then we hear the loving and urgent invitation: "Turn back, turn back from your evil ways; for why will you die, O house of Israel?" (Ezekiel 33:11).

It is lovely, to be sure, to see Jesus welcoming the children on his knee. And no doubt these excerpts from the judgment prophets lack that sense of innocence. But that is what makes God's love in those Old Testament passages even more compelling: it is precisely because the human audience is rebellious and undeserving that God's open-arms invitation is that much more dramatic.

We see this dramatic aspect of God's love in the Hebrew word *chesed*, used for God's love in the Old Testament. When the psalmist declares, "O give thanks to the LORD, for he is good / his steadfast love endures forever!" (Psalm 118:1), the word for "steadfast love" is *chesed*. When Miles Coverdale, who provided the first translation of the entire Bible into

English in 1535, came across this lovely Hebrew word, he couldn't find an adequate synonym in English. In order to compensate, Coverdale invented a word to describe God's love: *lovingkindness.*[11] So God's lovingkindness, which is so often associated with the New Testament, actually begins in the Old Testament.

The Continuity of God's Care for Us

Such is the nature of God's love: we struggle to find a word for it. Of course, that shouldn't be surprising. After all, we're trying to describe the very essence of God. Perhaps this is why the biblical writers often paint word pictures to help us "see" God; and when we see God, we see how much God cares for us.

One evening when I was ten years old, my mother was invited to speak at an event at a church across town and she invited me to come with her. When we arrived at the church where she was to speak, they found a Sunday school room where I could read, color, and play until the adult gathering was finished. I am grateful to God for that Sunday school room where they put me, for all these years later I can still remember a picture that was hanging on the wall of that room. It was not a spectacular piece of art, I suppose, but it was lovely. And it conveyed a message. It was a painting of Jesus as a good shepherd, surrounded by his flock. The sheep were peacefully gathered around him; one lamb was in his arms. There was green grass and a lovely brook. The sky was blue, and the overall mood of the picture was peaceful and serene.

They say that a child's heart—and perhaps an adult's too—is more likely to be captured through pictures than through words. Engage a child's imagination, and you can make an impression. And that's exactly what happened to me. That simple portrait of Jesus had an impact on my young heart. It drew me in, and I left that room understanding a little something more about my relationship with the Lord.

The painting was not mere sentiment, of course. It was a portrait based on a Scripture in which Jesus identified himself as "the good shepherd" (John 10). But careful students of the Bible know that Jesus was not inventing an image for himself. Rather, he was inserting himself into an image that had already existed in Israel's imagination for centuries. The concept of a good shepherd—and, specifically, the Lord as that Good Shepherd—had already been given full expression in the Old Testament.

We are well acquainted, of course, with the Twenty-Third Psalm, one of the best known and most loved passages in all the Bible. There the psalmist, himself once a shepherd, bore witness to the tender love, abiding presence, and provident care of God, illustrating those truths in terms of a shepherd's relationship to his sheep. And so when Jesus called himself the Good Shepherd, Psalm 23 may have been in view.

And Psalm 23 is not alone. Way back in Genesis, Jacob called God "the Shepherd" (49:24). The prophets Isaiah

(40:11), Jeremiah (31:10), and Micah (7:14) all allude to the Lord as the Shepherd of his people. And Ezekiel (chapter 34) features an extended message about the leaders of Israel being false and inadequate shepherds, so that God himself promises to become for them the Good Shepherd.

That Sunday school room presented me with a beautiful picture of Jesus, and it made an impression on me. I came away with a sense of the sweetness and strength of Jesus the Shepherd. And since that night, that picture has grown fuller and more beautiful for me as I have discovered its roots in so many Old Testament pictures of God as that loving Shepherd.

The Continuity of God's Relationship with Us

In the Bible we see the continuity of God's love through God's desire for us, God's open-arms invitation to us, and God's attentive care of us. Scripture also speaks specifically of God's relationship with us.

The psalmist famously called God his Shepherd, and it is a treasured image; but it is just one image in a much larger treasury. The psalmist also said that the Lord is a righteous judge (7:11), king (10:16), a rock, fortress, and deliverer (18:2), a refuge (46:1), redeemer (78:35), and savior (106:21).

Throughout all of Scripture we find this marvelous pattern of God revealed to us *relationally*. God is not unveiled in detached, philosophical, or theoretical language. Scripture does not settle for terms such as Force, Mind, or Being. Instead, from start to finish, the prevailing theme of God's self-revelation in the Bible is in relational terms and images. By relational terms, I mean those words that suggest natural counterparts. For example, if we say that God is Force, then what are we? The relationship is undefined and unclear. If, on the other hand, we say that God is our Shepherd, then we understand immediately what we are—those under God's guidance and protection—and what the relationship is. Likewise, we understand the relationship with Savior and Teacher, King, and Redeemer, and more.

Consequently, the testimony of Scripture does not simply help us to know about God—instead it invites us into relationship with God. And as a result, it encourages us to call God by certain kinds of titles, most of which are characterized by warmth and intimacy.

Perhaps the biblical images that suggest the deepest and most devoted kinds of love relationships with God are the husband-wife and parent-child imagery we find in both testaments. The New Testament concludes with an emphatic image of a marriage relationship between God and God's people (see Revelation 19:6-9; 21:2, 9; 22:17). This imagery draws from some of Jesus' parables, in which he implies his role as bridegroom (Matthew 25:1-13; Mark 2:18-19). More than the parables of Jesus, though, the theme of a husband-wife relationship between God and his people traces back to the Old Testament. In intimacy (Ezekiel 16:4-14), in covenant devotion (Hosea 3:19-23), and even in the face of infidelity (Jeremiah 3:1), the Lord is understood as a husband to his people.

Finally, the understanding of God as Father finds its fullest expression in the New Testament. There we see it in the light of the only-begotten Son, with whom we become joint heirs. Jesus the Son teaches us to pray by calling God, "Our Father" (Matthew 6:9), and the apostle assures us that, through our adoption into God's family, we have been given the right to call God "Papa" (Romans 8:15 *The Message*).

The truth of our parent-child relationship with God does not begin in the New Testament, however. The Old Testament prophet Isaiah prays,

> For you are our father,
>   though Abraham does not know us
>   and Israel does not acknowledge us;
> you, O LORD, are our father.
>
> (Isaiah 63:16)

The writers of Psalms (103:13) and Proverbs (3:12) make the comparison of God to a human father. And, most remarkably, the Lord himself poignantly expresses his father's heart for his people:

> I thought
>   how I would set you among my children,

94

and give you a pleasant land,
the most beautiful heritage of all the nations.
And I thought you would call me, My Father,
and would not turn from following me.

(Jeremiah 3:19)

When I was a brand new father, I asked my newborn daughter if she knew how much I loved her. She didn't. And neither do we comprehend how much God loves us. But make no mistake: God has been telling us of his love from the very beginning!

9

Finding True Love

Exploring a Few Scriptures that Can Confuse Us

We've seen that love is God's chief attribute, that it is God's very essence. And if that is true, then we may assume that everything God does is consistent with love. So what are we do to when we encounter Scripture in which God's words or deeds do not *seem* loving? It is a theological question, but it is also a deeply personal one.

Parents can somewhat understand this dilemma, for we know how often our own love is misunderstood by our children. For a good parent, love is the motivation for every no, as well as every yes. Love should be the impetus behind each punishment and imposed discipline. Yet in the moment of discipline, the child seldom recognizes the love. Indeed, he or she might think quite the opposite. How many times have I made my own children cry or made them angry? How many times has one of them stomped off in frustration? I do not pretend to be a perfect parent, but I guarantee you that always I love my children. And even though my wisdom has not been flawless, my heart has always been for their best. Yet they do not recognize everything I do as loving.

When we read in Scripture something about God that does not seem loving, we may be inclined to stomp off like a frustrated teenager. But instead I encourage us to look more closely and listen more carefully to those passages that often confuse us so that we can better understand God's true nature. This chapter is meant to help us with that.

Reclaiming the Word *Love*

In the early 1700s, Isaac Watts wrote a hymn that began, "Before Jehovah's awful throne."[12] Later that century, Charles Wesley, in his hymn about wrestling Jacob, included a line that read, "To me, to all, thy bowels move."[13] And in the 1880s, the familiar Christmas carol we know as "Deck the Halls" sang, "Don we now our gay apparel."

In these examples, we see how language changes over time. For Watts, *awful* still meant "awe inspiring." For Wesley, *bowels* were thought of as the seat of pity and tenderness. And in the late 1800s, *gay* simply meant "festive and cheerful."

So it is that, when we read that "God is love" (1 John 4:8), or when we speak of the love of God, we must be careful about our terms, for the meaning of *love* has changed in recent decades. Today's common usage of the word has diminished it to the point where it is, biblically speaking, hardly recognizable. Consider these expressions, any of which you may be apt to hear or even use during a typical week: *I love pizza. I love that restaurant. I love kittens. I love that song. I love sunny, spring days.*

Consider what the Apostle Paul offered to the Corinthians as perhaps the most famous definition of love:

> *Love is patient; love is kind; love is not*
> *envious or boastful or arrogant or rude.*
> *It does not insist on its own way; it is not*
> *irritable or resentful; it does not rejoice in*
> *wrongdoing, but rejoices in the truth. It*
> *bears all things, believes all things, hopes all*
> *things, endures all things. Love never ends.*
> *(1 Corinthians 13:4-8a)*

It would be hard to insert this classic, biblical definition of love into any of the previous uses, wouldn't it? It seems silly to ask myself, *Am I patient and kind with pizza? Do I not insist on my own way with that restaurant? Do I not keep a record of wrongs with spring days?*

If we could track all the times we hear and use the word *love* during an average week, it would be an interesting exercise to go back and find another way of expressing it in each instance. What was really meant? What was really being expressed? Often when we say we *love* something, we mean to say that we are enthusiastic about it or that we enjoy it. Sometimes *love* even becomes a synonym for *want*, as with the child who begs her mother for a puppy in the pet store, saying, "I just *love* puppies!" Yet enthusiasm, enjoyment, and wanting are not part of 1 Corinthians 13.

The case of the puppy is perhaps illustrative. The child begs for a puppy because she loves puppies, or so she claims. The mother, meanwhile, raises the practical questions of feeding, walking, bathing, training, and cleaning up after the pet. And in that conversation we see two different definitions of *love* at work. The child is talking about enthusiasm, enjoyment, and desire. The mother, meanwhile, is talking about effort, expense, and sacrificial care.

When we talk about God's love, then, we must be careful how we use the term. A somewhat childish definition has come to characterize our culture's use of the word, and we mustn't limit God to that sort of puppy love. God's love is the kind of love we read about in 1 Corinthians 13. It is the truest kind of love. It is the kind of sacrificial love that Jesus both described and exemplified: "Greater love has no one than this, that one lay down his life for his friends" (John 15:13 NASB).

Hidden Love

Sometimes the truth of God's love can be "hidden" in a Bible story or passage, and we must pray to have eyes to see it. Several years ago I led a year-long, through-the-Bible study with the folks in my church. We read the Bible cover to cover, with daily reading assignments for us as individuals and monthly meetings for us as a group. I encouraged the participants to write down questions as they read, and then we'd devote some time to discussing those questions together during our monthly group meetings.

When we were in the territory of Numbers and Deuteronomy, one of the most common questions was about Moses' fate. Actually, it was more of a complaint disguised as a question. "Why didn't God let Moses enter the Promised Land?" people asked. It seemed unfair. After all that Moses had done and had endured in his faithful service to God, why should he be denied that reward after what appeared to many to be so small an infractions? (see Numbers 20:8-12). And so we began to consider together the alternative.

When the Israelites crossed the Jordan River into the Promised Land—the step Moses was not allowed to take— what did they find there? Within a few miles, they would encounter the daunting walled city of Jericho. They famously conquered it, of course, but a battle was required.

As the Book of Joshua recounts the unfolding story, we watch the Israelites head up into the hill country of central Canaan. They attack, without success, the small town of Ai. After a discovery of sin in their midst and appropriate repentance, they try again to conquer Ai, and they succeed. Then there are more battles, one after another after another. Cities, towns, and villages; hills and valleys; foot soldiers, cavalry, and chariots.

Moses was 120 years old when he died. Before he died, he got to see the Promised Land as a whole, at a distance, as a panorama. But if he had been allowed to cross over, what would have been his view? He would not have been able to sit beneath his own vine and fig tree. Rather, he would have had to live through and lead the acre-by-acre conquest of the land.

When we watch the Israelites bid farewell to Moses, his left-behind fate seems unfair. In reality, however, I wonder if the Lord was doing him a great favor. They were heading off to do battle, while he got to enjoy the view. And we assume that he crossed over into a far more beautiful, bountiful, and eternal Promised Land, for which Canaan was only a poor foretaste.

Frederick W. Faber, a clergyman in nineteenth-century England, wrote a number of hymns, the most famous and enduring of which is probably "Faith of Our Fathers." A personal favorite of mine, meanwhile, begins with this verse:

"There's a wideness in God's mercy, like the wideness of the sea; there's a kindness in God's justice, which is more than liberty."[14] I don't know what lovely, personal experience may have led Faber to that insight about God's justice, but I am reminded of it each time I read Moses' story.

It was the justice of God that prevented Moses from entering the Promised Land. Yet upon further review, we see that God's justice was, in fact, a kindness to Moses. What is generally billed as judgment, therefore, was clearly an act of love.

The Flyswatter Principle

A bit of logic can help us see God's love behind what, on the surface, might read as judgment. When reading the Bible cover to cover, we come to a long stretch of judgment messages. From the Book of Isaiah to the Book of Zephaniah—with only a few exceptions—we find chapter after chapter, book after book, of judgment prophecies. This is heavy reading. The descriptions of the people's sins are troubling, and the subsequent portraits of God's impending judgment because of those sins are truly horrifying. If our fondest pictures from Scripture are the Lord as Shepherd and Jesus with the children around his knees, then we may find this voluminous judgment material unpleasant and unsettling. Yet the judgment prophecies are every bit as much an expression of the love of God as the Twenty-Third Psalm.

We catch a glimpse of that love in the midst of one of the most miserable judgment prophets. God instructed the prophet Jeremiah to commit God's messages to writing, saying, "Take a scroll and write on it all the words that I have spoken to you against Israel and Judah and all the nations, from the day I spoke to you, from the days of Josiah until today." (Jeremiah 36:2).

This moment offers a rare glimpse into the creation of the written word of God, which we have and cherish today. But it is the Lord's expressed purpose for that scroll that is truly revealing: "It may be that when the house of Judah hears of all the disasters that I intend to do to them, all of them may turn from their evil ways, so that I may forgive their iniquity and their sin" (Jeremiah 36:3).

All of those painful chapters of judgment messages, you see, are gracious in their purpose. Even though the tone is severe and the content is harsh, the heart is all loving. And if we do not recognize the heart, we will not fully understand the words.

Theodoret was a monk and bishop from Syria who became an influential theologian in the fifth-century church. In commenting on the judgment messages in the Old Testament prophet Hosea, Theodoret makes a logical connection between God's threats and God's love: "The reason that the God of all threatens punishment, you see, is not to inflict it on those he threatens but to strike them with fear and lead them to repentance, and by ridding them of their wicked behavior extend to them salvation. After all, if he wanted to punish, he would not threaten punishment; instead, by threatening he makes clear that he longs to save and not to punish."[15]

When I was in fourth grade, flies invaded our school building. I'm sure it was a great irritation to the teachers, for the flies were constantly buzzing about heads and landing on desks. To a group of us boys, however, it was a real source of entertainment. In fact, we had weekly competitions to see who could kill the most flies. We kept our "trophies" in the pencil trays of our desks until each Friday, when it was time to clean out our desks. Then we would tally the dead flies to declare a winner for the week.

Here is one thing I know about fly swatting: you don't warn the fly. If your purpose is to kill it, then you sneak up on it very slowly, preferably from behind. You certainly don't make a big fuss to let it know that you're there and that you're coming.

This is the pragmatic logic behind Theodoret's insight. And the pragmatic logic leads to gospel truth. If the Lord's ultimate will was to destroy the people, the Lord would not tell them that he was going to destroy them. And so the abundance of judgment messages in the Old Testament is a reflection of both the volume of the people's sinfulness and the still greater measure of God's grace and love—the true love of a Perfect Parent.

The Love of a Perfect Parent

We are fond of the phrase *true love*. It's a way of affirming the beauty and significance of what we've found and experienced in some relationship. By adding the word *true*, it becomes an emphatic way of saying *love*.

At the same time, the expression raises a fascinating possibility. If there is true love, then might the opposite also exist? If some love is true, does that mean that other love is false? *False* seems like a dramatic assessment—perhaps a stronger word than we are willing to use. Still, every thinking person would acknowledge that not all love is equal. And perhaps many of us have been the victims of some terribly inadequate love along the way.

We know that if something is valuable, it is susceptible to counterfeiting. If a currency, a work of art, or a consumer product has value and appeal, then someone somewhere is likely to produce a fake version of it—a knock-off, a forgery, a counterfeit. And if that is true in the material world, perhaps we shouldn't be surprised when the phenomenon is also found in relational and spiritual realms. So if love has such profound value, then we should expect that it invites counterfeiting. Perhaps that's why we need to use the phrase *true love*—because we know instinctively that there is also false love.

The Bible is impeccably wise about love. It celebrates the passionate and sensual love so freely expressed in the Song of Solomon. It knows all about the romantic love that makes seven years pass as though they were a few days (Genesis 29:20). It is unsurprised by the counterfeit love that turns so quickly into hate (2 Samuel 13:15). And it insists on the fundamentally sacrificial nature of true love (John 15:13; 1 Corinthians 13:4-7).

We also discover that the Bible is unapologetic about the discipline that comes with parental love. "Those who spare the rod hate their children," declares the ancient wise man, "but those who love them are diligent to discipline them" (Proverbs 13:24). And that's not just an Old Testament mentality, for the writer of Hebrews applies it to our relationship to God: "for the Lord disciplines those whom he loves" (Hebrews 12:6). And Jesus himself declares, "I reprove and discipline those whom I love" (Revelation 3:19).

Every parent knows what it is to have his or her love be misunderstood. So often, our children do not recognize our love. Indeed, at times, they might think the opposite. And so it is that God, the Perfect Parent, suffers the same fate with us. Yet as the whole of Scripture supports, we can read God's Word with the assurance that when we are dealing with God, we are dealing with true love.

10

Heaven's Mission Statement

Identifying the Continuity of God's Purpose and Plan

We are beginning to see the pattern develop before our eyes. God is not different in the Old Testament than in the New Testament after all. Both testaments faithfully bear witness to the divine nature. God's character does not change. And neither, we discover, does God's purpose.

A story is told about a minister who was spending several months in Israel. He leased a car for the duration of his visit, and when he ran into some car trouble, he went to a local mechanic. The minister watched as the Israeli mechanic tinkered under the hood and then started the engine, only to turn it off again and tinker some more. Finally, the mechanic started the engine once again, and it sounded the way it was supposed to sound. The mechanic happily exclaimed something in Hebrew, triumphantly shut the hood, and settled up with the minister.

As the clergyman drove away, he kept reflecting on the Hebrew word that he heard the mechanic exclaim. He recognized it vaguely from his seminary days, but he couldn't place it. Then, finally, it dawned on him: the mechanic had exclaimed, "Righteous!"

That may seem to us like a strange interjection, but it offers a helpful insight into the biblical understanding of righteousness. A thing is righteous, you see, when it is functioning the way it was designed to function. Accordingly, when the engine has been fine-tuned so that it is sounds and runs the way it was meant to, that is righteousness. We might not describe the purring engine as righteous, but we would come close; for we might say, "Now that sounds just right!"

A person doesn't need to be especially devout or have any theological training to understand biblical righteousness. One only needs to be a bit of a pragmatist. In day-to-day living, we know the difference between things that function the way they were designed to and things that do not. The former give us great pleasure, while the latter are a burden to us. And if we create something that functions the way it's meant to, it is a source of pride and satisfaction for us. But if it doesn't work properly, we are deeply disappointed. The heartache of the creator is far more profound than the mere frustration of the consumer.

The biblical story of Creation reveals a God who creates everything just right. Each day of the Creation event is punctuated by God's pleasure in its goodness: "God saw everything that he had made, and indeed, it was very good" (Genesis 1:31). But very shortly thereafter, as the story goes, that goodness is damaged. It is not utterly destroyed, for true goodness is more durable than that. But something was profoundly broken. And as we will see, God's central purpose throughout Scripture is to restore what has been broken—to restore it to righteousness

A Tale of Two Desks

When I was a young boy, my family had a small cottage near a lake where we spent several weeks together each summer. It was humble and musty, but lovely, and we all cherished that house and the time together there. My bedroom in that house was quite modest—all it could hold was a bed, a dresser, and a small secretary desk. Those few pieces of furniture were constants in all my years in that summer cottage. Eventually that house was sold, and most of its furnishings stayed with the house. We had, after all, everything we needed in our own year-round home. But I was happily surprised one day when my mother presented to me that old desk from my childhood. She had claimed it from the house before it was sold, and she had arranged for it to be refinished and made into a more handsome piece, suitable for an adult. I have it still in my study at home, and I cherish it.

Interestingly, just a very few years ago, my wife happened upon an almost identical desk at a rummage sale. The price was too good to resist, and so she picked it up for one of our children's bedrooms. It was used briefly by one of our daughters and was then relegated to our basement when she outgrew it.

Here, then, is a hypothetical question. If the rummage-sale desk broke, what would I do with it? I'd probably throw it out. But what if my childhood desk was the one that was broken? What would I do? I'd probably make every effort to mend and restore it.

To an outside observer, there would be little or no difference between the two desks. My reason for repairing the one and discarding the other would not be apparent to the naked eye. But for me, the choice would be simple and obvious. Even if the two desks were identical, one has tremendous personal value to me and the other has almost none. And so I fix the one but not the other.

You and I face this kind of choice routinely. Every few days, we are presented with some decision about whether a thing should be fixed or tossed. And most of the time, that decision is made based on value. If an item is worth a lot—

financially, sentimentally, functionally, or whatever—then we make the effort to fix it. If, however, the item is not worth much to us, then we are more apt to give up on it rather than invest time and resources in repairing it.

When we choose to fix a broken thing, we are making a statement about that thing's value. In the case of the childhood desk, its value is that I love it. And so, likewise, it is a testament to the love of God that the Creator did not discard creation when it broke. Instead, God invested in fixing what was broken. The God who made things right at the beginning continues to work to make things right—from Genesis to Revelation.

God's Plan to Make Things Right

Sometimes in a pastoral counseling setting, I will ask a person, "What's your perfect picture?" I find that this is a helpful, clarifying question for some, as it enables them to set aside past patterns and present obstacles, freeing them up to express the deep desires of their hearts.

Likewise, if we could see God's perfect picture, we would understand the deep desires of God's heart. And we are most fortunate in this regard, for Scripture gives us many glimpses of that perfect picture. We see it in Eden at the beginning and in the New Jerusalem at the end. We see it in the prophecy of the peaceable kingdom, the articulation of the new covenant, and so many promises of the Messiah. And through each instance, we get to peek into God's heart.

Meanwhile, we get another glimpse of the Lord's "perfect picture" in an unexpected place. The Old Testament Law is not as descriptive of the Book of Revelation or as poetic as Isaiah, but still it paints an important picture, for the Law articulates God's will. It gives expression to how God wants life to be lived, both individually and communally. Perhaps most precious of all, the Law shows us God's perfect will in an imperfect world.

This is an important distinction from, say, the garden of Eden or the New Jerusalem, which depict perfect places. The Law, by contrast, speaks into the midst of an obviously imperfect world, and it endeavors to work with flawed and fallen people. And through it all, we see the persistent heart of God that wants everything to be just right.

Leslie Weatherhead, who served as a pastor in London during World War II, preached a series of sermons to his congregation on the subject of God's will that were combined into a slender volume titled *The Will of God*, which has sold over a million copies. Over the course of those helpful chapters, Weatherhead suggests a way of thinking about God's will that he calls "the circumstantial will of God." Weatherhead assumes that there was an original will of God for humankind, which was perfect. It is characterized by the unblemished goodness of Eden. Likewise, Weatherhead affirms that there is an "ultimate will of God," which is also perfect, and which will be achieved in the end. In between, however, is "the circumstantial will of God—God's plan within certain circumstances."[16]

What Weatherhead recognized was that, in a fallen world of sinful human beings, God's perfect will is not always done. Neither, however, is that perfect will ultimately thwarted. Instead, God's circumstantial will is at work even within the context of our imperfection. A golfer might think of the sand wedge as an emblem of the circumstantial will of God— having your ball in the sand is not the ideal, but that club is designed to help get it out.

The Old Testament Law is an expression of God's circumstantial will. Given the context of an imperfect people in an imperfect world, the Law spelled out how the people of Israel should live their lives. The Law doesn't pretend there are no enemies, but it stipulates how enemies should be treated. It doesn't assume there will be no poor, no widows, no orphans, but it seeks to guarantee justice and mercy for all of them.

The Law also bears witness to God's desire to redeem. As I already noted in my story about the two desks, we tend to set aside or throw away the broken things that we do not value. But we seek to repair the broken item that is important to us. So it is that God, who made things right in the beginning, continues to want to make things right in the midst of brokenness. And the justice system prescribed in the Law was the divine antidote to what was wrong in society.

Punishment for offenders, restitution for victims, correction of injustice and oppression—these were all built into the Law's design. They were God's instructions to make right whatever was wrong in the land. It is an early glimpse of C. S. Lewis's point about God's will: Christianity "thinks that a great many things have gone wrong with the world that God made and that God insists, and insists very loudly, on our putting them right again."[17] The emphasis on Law in the Old Testament points to God's desire and plan to make things right.

Justice's Cousin, Judgment

God not only desires to make things right again but is willing to intervene in order to do so. The dual meaning of an ancient Hebrew word illustrates this well.

It's helpful to know that Hebrew words are generally based on roots comprised of just a few consonants. All the changes and nuances in meaning, then, come with prefixes, suffixes, and changing vowels between those consonants—which brings us to the interesting case of the root *mshpt*. When the prophet Micah famously declared what the Lord requires, he listed three fundamentals: "to do justice, and to love kindness, / and to walk humbly with your God" (Micah 6:8). The underlying Hebrew word that we translate "justice" comes from that Hebrew root: *mshpt*. That is what God wants us to do: justice.

Meanwhile, in the writings of the prophet Hosea, we hear a warning to the northern kingdom about the punishment God has in store for them. Hosea says, "Ephraim is oppressed, crushed in judgment, / because he was determined to go after vanity" (Hosea 5:11). Hosea's word that we translate "judgment" is also from the Hebrew *mshpt.*

The same basic word, you see, means both justice and judgment. It is applied both to the corrective action that we human beings are expected to take in society (*justice*) and to the destructive retribution of God (*judgment*). Justice and judgment are close cousins. In one sense, *mshpt* suggests exactly the same thing in both instances. Whether the functioning of a society's justice system or the calamitous intervention of God, the purpose remains the same—to guarantee that everything is made right, which includes deliberate action to correct or eradicate whatever is wrong.

We gather from the narrative flow of Scripture that the one use of *mshpt* compensates for the other. In other words, when human justice fails, divine judgment becomes necessary. To put it in everyday terms, if I properly police myself as a driver, then it will not be necessary for a police officer to pull me over for speeding or some other violation. It's when I fail to do everything right as a driver that an external force must intervene in order to make things right.

This is a theme that pulses through the Old Testament prophets. Among Amos's audience, for example, human justice has failed. Sin has run amok in the form of idolatry, greed, oppression, and hypocrisy, and it has gone uncorrected. Neither the civic nor spiritual leaders of the land have taken responsibility for restoring justice. And so Amos warns the people about the coming judgment of God.

The principles that we see at work for the nation of Israel in the Old Testament are also at work in the church in the New Testament. In the letters of Paul, for example, we observe the corrective action that the apostle takes in order to make things right in Corinth, Galatia, Colossae, and Thessalonica. In Corinth, he calls for the excommunication of a church member (1 Corinthians 5:3-5). For the Thessalonians, he lays out policies for dealing with the lazy ones in their midst (2 Thessalonians 3:6-12). And to the Galatians, he warns about false teaching in the strongest possible terms (1:8-9).

Finally, at the end of the New Testament, we observe the same corrective messages and methods at work in Jesus' words to several of the seven churches of Revelation. He speaks correction to those individuals, groups, and churches who tolerate wrong living or wrong believing in their midst. He encourages them to rectify their situations and warns of the judgment awaiting those who do not make things right. Of course, there is a limit to how much we sinful human beings can do to make things right. Happily, the Lord himself has chosen to intervene in order to make *us* right!

The One Who Makes Us Right

At Creation, the Lord made everything right. And it seems that the pinnacle of that creation, nearest to God's heart and made in God's image, were human beings. Ironically, we are the culprits who did wrong and compromised the rightness of what God had made. So it is that the salvation offered in Christ is God's plan to make us right.

My father was a pastor, and I grew up watching him write his sermons on an old, manual Royal typewriter, with a carriage that dinged and keys that would stick. By the time I was learning to type, the typewriters were electric. And by the time I was in seminary, I used a word processor. I thought writing couldn't get any easier.

Justified text—in which a line or block of text is flush with both the left and right margins—used to be the sole province of professionally printed publications. On the old manual typewriter, of course, the text was naturally flush with the left margin. The right margin, however, was a real hodgepodge of longer and shorter lines of print. The effect of justifying, then, is that a line of text that would not, by itself, make it to the right margin is extended so that it reaches that margin. To justify the text, therefore, is to help it be what it is not. Quite literally, to justify text is to make it "right."

This is an everyday illustration of a gospel truth. Indeed, it is more explicit in the language of the New Testament than in our own. The truth is that through Christ, we are justified: that is, we are made right.

Justification may not be a word that remains prominent in our vocabulary. It is prominent in the gospel message, however. And it is one of the several important words that come under the broad umbrella of salvation, along with sanctification, regeneration, atonement, and reconciliation. If we forfeit the vocabulary of the gospel, we may lose touch with some of the truth of the gospel. Taken together, these meaningful terms bear witness to that breadth of ways that God makes us right. We are restored to right relationship with our Creator. The righteousness of Christ is imputed to us. And the sanctifying work of the Spirit makes us more and more right in the sense that the Israeli mechanic understood: that is, we function increasingly the way we were designed to function.

The Apostle Paul had to remind the Christians in Galatia about the truly gracious nature of the gospel. They had fallen again into a common and natural rut of relying on works and rituals in order to be in a right relationship with God. And so Paul explained to them the truth of justification by faith in Christ, including this: "Now it is evident that no one is justified before God by the law; for 'The one who is righteous will live by faith'" (Galatians 3:11). In that English translation, a compelling part of the truth goes undetected. But in the original Greek, we recognize the fuller beauty of the message.

When Paul says that no one is justified by the Law, the Greek verb he uses for justified is *dikaioo*. Then, when he cites the prophet Habakkuk, saying, "the one who is righteous will live by faith," the Greek adjective for righteous is *dikaios*. The semantic relationship of the words bears witness to the relationship between the two—justification and righteousness go hand in hand. The one leads to the other.

The righteousness of God is apparent from beginning to end of Scripture. It is the manifest will of God at Creation, as well as the promised culmination at the end of the age. And in between we see that the God who made things right from the start continues to make right the things that have gone wrong.

Mercifully, that includes us. God engages us in the redemptive process of making things right in this world. And in Christ, God works to make us right ourselves. The Lord is not willing for this broken world to remain broken—corrupt, fallen, sinful. And so we rejoice in the truth that we "are now justified by his grace as a gift, through the redemption that is in Christ Jesus" (Romans 3:24).

11

Same God, Different People

Recognizing Who Has Changed

So, *are* there differences between the Old and New Testaments? Yes, of course, but as we've discussed in the preceding chapters, those differences aren't what you might expect. What we've discovered thus far is the overwhelming unity of Scripture and the consistency of God's nature in both testaments despite their differences.

If we are drawn to the loving and relational nature of God that we see in Jesus, we should feel very much at home in the

Old Testament. Why? Because all of the relational language for God originates there. God's desire for forgiveness, atonement, and reconciliation are all manifested there. And the divine insistence on love, compassion, and justice are all part of the Law and the Prophets.

Likewise, if we are challenged by the no-nonsense holiness of God that characterizes so many laws and stories in the Old Testament, we will recognize the same challenge pulsing through the New Testament. Indeed, we are challenged as followers of Christ to be equally no-nonsense. The early church was called to be forthright with sin in the midst of the community, and the disciples were taught to be quick and decisive in dealing with the causes of sin in their individual lives.

In both the holiness and the love of God, we discover the coherence of the One who makes things right. From creation through redemption, in both law and gospel, in both judgment and forgiveness, this is the will and purpose of God. God made things right from the start. In the midst of the world's brokenness, God still works to make things right. The cross of Christ is the ultimate symbol of that truth. And in both Old and New Testaments, we see grand portraits of how the Lord will make things right again in the end.

In short, the character of God does not change throughout the pages of Scripture. The will and purpose of God do not change from one testament to the next. The differences between the testaments, therefore, must be traced elsewhere. And in order to counteract the rumor, then trace them we must.

The computer in my office at church was recently replaced. It was a process, of course, to transfer all contents and settings. And after the digital transition was complete, there was the physical switch. I had to remove the old computer, which meant crouching down into a small cubbyhole under my desk where all the electrical connections reside. What I thought would be a straightforward task—unplugging my computer—turned out to require some detective work, for what I found hidden beneath and behind my desk was a great web of electrical cords. One was for the computer, but there were also cords for the printer, the docking station, the external speakers, two monitors, and so forth. In order to remove the correct plug, I had to trace each cord back to its source.

So it is with our present enterprise. There *are* differences between the testaments. But in the tangle of many issues and factors, we should be careful to trace those differences back to the right source. The two common tendencies, as we have noted, are to attribute the differences either to a change in God or an inadequacy in Scripture. But we are pulling on the wrong cords. The real change between the testaments is found elsewhere.

A Changing People

We have captured the perception of the differences between the Old and New Testaments with the question, "When did God become a Christian?" The root cause of many seeming differences between the two testaments, however, is not that God became a Christian, at all, but rather that God's people did. In saying that, I am not referring to a conversion of individuals. Rather, the point is that a change occurs in the very kind of group that is identified as the people of God in the one testament and in the other.

In both the Old Testament and the New Testament, you see, God has a people. This is, incidentally, one of the points of continuity between the two sections of the Bible. In both cases, God makes a sovereign choice of a people with whom and through whom God will work.

The pattern begins with Abraham. Even before there is a "people" to choose, God begins the process with this demographically unpromising individual. The Lord is the one who makes the promises and articulates boldly improbable promises for Abraham and his yet-to-be descendants. Generations pass, and those descendants of Abraham become known by different names at different times. During the early years, before they have a land of their own, they are referred to as Hebrews. Later, and for much of Old Testament history, they are the nation of Israel. Then, following the division of the twelve tribes and the eradication of the northern tribes, the terminology shifts again. The dominant remaining tribe was Judah, from which we get the word *Jew*. That is the word employed for the people of God toward the end of Old Testament history.

The New Testament, meanwhile, bears witness to a new covenant that applies to both Jews and Gentiles who place their faith in Christ. Our purpose here is not to try to resolve the question of the status of unbelieving Jews in God's plan. Paul struggles with that question, and suggests that they are branches cut off (Romans 11:17ff), while also affirming that "the gifts and the calling of God are irrevocable" (11:29). What is clear, however, is that the New Testament portrays followers of Jesus as ones chosen by the Lord (John 15:16; 1 Peter 2:9), partners in a new covenant (2 Corinthians 3:5-6), true descendants of Abraham (Galatians 3), and the instruments of God's work in the world (Mark 16:15).

This difference between what we might call the Old Testament people of God and the New Testament people of God has dramatic ramifications. The shift in emphasis, you see, is from a nation to a church. And that carries implications at two important levels.

First, a nation is physically defined by land. A land has borders, which probably have to be defended. A nation is apt to have enemies, and therefore wars. So we discover that stories of international conflict form a large part of the Old Testament narrative. We read about many battles and numerous casualties. War, literally, comes with the territory.

The New Testament seems comparatively free of such carnage, but then the New Testament also covers a fraction of the time that Old Testament history represents. It was written during a time of relative peace under the unified Roman Empire. And, most significantly, the church at this time is not a nation with borders and battles, but an international body that endeavors to cross all borders. Has God changed, then, from the war-torn Old Testament to the relatively peaceful, seemingly pacifist New Testament? I think not. In fact, we will see the continuity between the testaments on this point in the next section. But while God does not change, the community of God's people does.

Second, a nation must have a criminal justice system. Israel is a civil society, and so it must have a means for redressing wrongs and for punishing criminals. Consequently, we read in both the stipulations of the Law and in the stories from Israel's history a great deal about offenses and their penalties. And we are particularly struck by the prevalence of the death penalty. Indeed, with a little research, we will discover that the first seven of the Ten Commandments can all be connected to capital offenses in the Old Testament justice system. All in all, it seems to us like a lot of killing. In some cases, the death penalty is invoked for behaviors that are not considered crimes at all in our day (for example, misusing God's name, working on the Sabbath, or cursing one's parents). And all of this seems quite severe, while the New Testament appears to be much more forgiving.

But again, the New Testament audience is a different one. Jesus and Paul are not giving instructions for how a nation should order its society. Rather, there are the individual ethics—how one ought to live his or her life—and the teachings about how the church ought to operate. In neither case, though, is there authority involved for implementing criminal justice. It's simply not an issue.

We hear Jesus teaching us to turn the other cheek (Matthew 5:39) and to forgive again and again (Matthew 18:21-22). We see him dismissing the woman caught in the act of adultery (John 8:2-11). And we read Paul's challenge to the Corinthians that they would be better off being wronged than suing one another for their rights (1 Corinthians 6:1-8). Yet it would be an insult to the New Testament's sense of justice to suggest that those kinds of individual ethics should be employed by a nation. The courts would not be just if they turn the other cheek to a thief. The society would not be pleasing God if it "forgives" a murderer and lets him or her go free. On the contrary, Paul affirms that civil authority comes from God and serves God's purpose. And the official "is the servant of God to execute wrath on the wrongdoer" (Romans 13:4).

Still, since the dominant context of the Old Testament is a nation and the audience for New Testament teachings is individual believers and the church, we come away from the two testaments with different tastes in our mouths. The Old seems harsh, marked by battles and bloodshed. The New, in contrast, seems peaceful and marked by forgiveness. But let us translate the will of God from the one context to the other, and we will hear the New echoing the Old.

A Changing Struggle

"Our struggle is not against flesh and blood," Paul declared (Ephesians 6:12 NASB). Right away, that's different from the Old Testament situation. The ancient nation of Israel had to engage in numerous flesh-and-blood battles. But the church of the New Testament was quickly an international body. It did not have land and borders, and so it did not face the type of conflicts that mark so much of Israel's history.

The church had different conflicts, however. The Apostle Paul's counsel to the Christians in Ephesus is not that there are no struggles or enemies. Rather, he explains that they are not flesh-and-blood struggles, but rather they are battles "against the rulers, against the authorities, against the cosmic powers of this present darkness, against the spiritual forces of evil in the heavenly places" (Ephesians 6:12). Paul is unblushing, therefore, in borrowing from the imagery of military conflict to describe the situation and articulate the need. He recommends spiritual armor to the believers (6:10-17). Faith, righteousness, and truth are not conventional weaponry, to be sure, but as Charles Wesley put it, they are what you must "take to arm you for the fight."[18]

Paul's "armor of God" is part of a larger paradigm that permeates the New Testament. We are introduced to it with the preaching of John the Baptist early in Matthew, and we see it come to a climax with the final battle in Revelation. All four Gospel writers report the ministry of John the Baptist. And when Matthew introduces John to us, he characterizes John's message thus: "In those days John the Baptist appeared in the wilderness of Judea, proclaiming, 'Repent, for the kingdom of heaven has come near'" (Matthew 3:1-2). And so we are confronted from the start of the New Testament with a kingdom paradigm.

The magi and Pilate both assumed that Jesus came to be king of the Jews. Even the disciples thought the issue was the kingdom of Israel. But the shift has been made from a land with borders to a different sort of kingdom: "the kingdom of heaven has come near."

One chapter later, we meet a new layer. "The devil took [Jesus] to a very high mountain and showed him all the kingdoms of the world and their splendor; and he said to him, 'All these I will give you, if you will fall down and worship me'" (Matthew 4:8-9). Now we understand better the magnitude of what John the Baptist was declaring. If "all the kingdoms of the world" are the devil's to give, then the coming of God's kingdom into this world is a watershed event.

Kingdom language pervades the teaching of Jesus. It is so prominent, in fact, that we may not notice it right before our eyes. I'm thinking of the Lord's Prayer, which is just sixty-six words, yet Jesus mentions the kingdom twice within that brevity: "Thy kingdom come" (Matthew 6:10 KJV) and "Thine is the kingdom" (Matthew 6:13 KJV).

The juxtaposition of kingdoms in this world suggests a conflict. The language of conflict is reflected in references to "the enemy" (Luke 10:19) and the "adversary" (1 Timothy 5:14; 1 Peter 5:8). And the Revelation letters to the churches of Ephesus, Smyrna, Pergamum, Thyatira, Sardis, Philadelphia, and Laodicea all feature promises to those who "conquer." Each of the seven churches had its own unique situation, yet all of them had this in common: they were engaged in a conflict, and they were challenged to overcome.

"After John was arrested, Jesus came to Galilee, proclaiming the good news of God, and saying, 'The time is fulfilled, and the kingdom of God has come near'" (Mark 1:14-15). The Lord had established his beachhead into enemy territory, you see. It is like when Joshua's troops crossed into Canaan, except that this was a spiritual and eternal business. And so, while we sense that there is a great deal more carnage in the Old Testament than in the New, there is no less warfare in the New.

The New Testament calls followers of Christ to engage in spiritual battle. It's an ongoing conflict, with or without our assent, with or without our conscious participation. It's not against flesh and blood, as it was for ancient Israel, but a constant struggle nonetheless. Yet just as God guided and equipped the Israelite nation as they encountered their many foes, God continues to guide and equip us today for the spiritual battles we face.

The Big Picture

Even when we understand the difference between nation and church, the Old Testament events can still feel severe to us. We are uneasy with how the Law treats some things that offend us as minor or perhaps not even wrong at all. And we come away from certain laws and some stories with a sense of a trigger-happy Deity. Many sinners are sentenced to death by the divinely imposed system of the Law, and some are struck down by God directly with a frightening immediacy.

We often set this in contrast to the cherished episode in John's Gospel where Jesus is presented with a woman who had been caught in adultery (John 8:2-7). Our understanding of the Old Testament Law tells us that she should have been stoned to death, and that is what the antagonists in the episode assert. But far from a divine judgment, Jesus intervenes to prevent even the human judgment. And that, we suspect, encapsulates the difference between the Old and New Testaments.

Let us pull back the lens a bit, however, to see a bigger picture and the pattern within it.

Consider, for example, the strange story of Achan (see Joshua 7). At the time that the Israelites invaded the land of Canaan and conquered the city of Jericho, Achan willfully disobeyed the Lord's instruction not to keep any spoils of war from the city by taking and hiding some gold and silver from the battlefield. The community didn't know what Achan had done until they were defeated in their next battle. The Lord explained to the bewildered Joshua that Israel was unable to stand against its enemy because of the sin in their midst. And so Achan was identified and executed.

The episode seems harsh to us at several levels, yet we see the same principle at work in the New Testament. Paul expressed profound dismay that the Corinthians were tolerating sexual immorality in their midst. It wasn't that the whole church—or even many within the church—were misbehaving. It was just one man. Yet Paul insisted that "he who has done this [should] have been removed from among you" (1 Corinthians 5:2). And so the apostle passes dramatic judgment: "You are to hand this man over to Satan for the destruction of the flesh" (v. 5).

A church and a nation are very different contexts, but we see how the same principle translates across the two contexts. The people of God are not to tolerate sin in their midst: they must eradicate it. And what is true communally is also true individually, for Jesus says, "If your right eye causes you to sin, tear it out and throw it away....And if your right hand causes you to sin, cut it off and throw it away"

(Matthew 5:29, 30). When the Lord chastises the church at Thyatira, he says, "I have this against you: you tolerate that woman Jezebel, who calls herself a prophet and is teaching and beguiling my servants to practice fornication and to eat food sacrificed to idols" (Revelation 2:20). The condemnation was not for what the church itself was practicing or believing, but only for what it was tolerating in its midst. And so, just as the Old Testament Law required the nation of Israel to keep itself pure from evil in its midst, the church in the New Testament was to be equally no-nonsense.

We make a mistake when we think that to be intolerant is to be unforgiving. The line between tolerance and forgiveness has been blurred. Indeed, the blur can become so pervasive that forgiveness is marginalized altogether. That is to say, when forgiveness is associated with tolerance, soon tolerance morphs into acceptance, and acceptance can come to mean that there is nothing that needs to be forgiven.

God is forgiving, but God is not tolerant. He is patient with sinners, but not accepting of sin. And if we recognize sin as not only offensive to God's nature but also injurious to ours, we will rejoice in that intolerance. It is the stuff of grace.

We see the perfect will of God manifested in Jesus' encounter with the adulterous woman. There is forgiveness of sin, but no tolerance for sin. "Neither do I condemn you," he says to the woman he has set free. "Go your way, and from now on do not sin again" (John 8:11). As we've already noted, God is committed to restoring us to righteousness—to fixing that which has been broken. Sometimes the discipline that comes with restoration can seem difficult and uncomfortable. Yet Scripture consistently reminds us that God has our best in mind, and so we learn to trust the Lord as our Perfect Parent.

Consistency Amidst the Differences

I have five children, all girls. At this moment, the oldest is twenty-two and the youngest is three. From time to time, I find myself telling each of them to be careful. But what "careful" looks like varies with age because there are, of course, tremendous differences between a young adult and a toddler. Yet, at some core level, there is no difference in what I want for them. I want what is best for them—at every age. And part of my heart's desire for the children I love can be expressed in the same phrase at every age and stage: "Be careful." It means different things at different times, but it is always my will and my counsel.

What we understand instinctively as parents can be applied to our reading of Scripture. The people of God in the Old Testament and in the New Testament are living in very different contexts. A nation and a church are even more distinct than a toddler and an adult. Yet God's will for them is consistent across time and space.

As we read the two testaments, we must bear in mind the differences between the people with whom God is dealing, the audiences to whom God is speaking. Yes, there are differences between the testaments. But if we look carefully, we'll discover that the differences reside with the people, not with the Lord. God's character, will, and style are the same, and when we can view both testaments through this lens, it enriches and expands our relationship with the Lord.

12

Nothing New About the Sun

Considering How an Eternal God Is Unchanging

In the church building where my middle-school daughter attends school, there is a wall featuring confirmation class pictures dating back to the 1940s. My daughter is mystified by how long I can stand there and study those pictures. Of particular interest to me is the series of pictures that range from the confirmation class of 1974 to the confirmation class of 2004. The same man was pastor of that church for all of those years, and so he appears in every picture. It is a fascinating exercise to watch the aging process recorded in that subtle but undeniable way. There is no single year when one might say, "Boy, does he ever look older than the previous year!" Yet over the course of the series of pictures, the pastor transforms from a young man into an old man.

As does every human being, I, too, change over time. Long-term changes can be chronicled like the photographs I see in that church hallway. But I also discover that, in the short term, how I feel can change dramatically from one day to the next. One morning I wake up feeling robust and able to take on all challenges. The next morning, for no reason I can trace, I am fragile and easily discouraged.

Yes, human beings change over time. But our God is different. God declares, "I the Lord do not change" (Malachi 3:6). And that may be, in part, because God has a different relationship to time.

One of the fundamental affirmations we make is that God is eternal. But what is the relationship between eternity and time? Because we are limited naturally to what we know, we tend to slip into thinking of eternity as simply a very long time, or perhaps even never-ending time. But what if it is something more than that? What if eternity stands completely outside of time? If so, then God cannot change over time, for God does not exist within time. When God says to Moses, "I am who I am" (Exodus 3:14), that name may be making a statement about God's eternal nature—and that has dramatic implications for our understanding of the God of both testaments.

God Doesn't Change, Except When He Does

I grew up in a church that had very formal worship services. The sanctuary was large and Gothic, which lent itself to formality, and everything about how the service was conducted was designed to fit in. In that setting, I remember that the Scripture readings had a distinctive style. The reading was serious and sonorous. It reflected, I think, a certain understanding of reverence; but rather than reading a passage with a tone of excitement or of sadness, with the sound of rejoicing or of scolding, every passage was read aloud in the same way.

That's not how the Bible was written, of course. The psalmist says, "Praise him with clanging cymbals; / praise him with loud clashing cymbals!" (Psalm 150:5). Job cried out, "I loathe my life; / I will give free utterance to my complaint; / I will speak in the bitterness of my soul" (Job 10:1). And Jesus invites, "Come to me, all you that are weary and are carrying heavy burdens, and I will give you rest" (Matthew 11:28). Each of these Scriptures has a very different kind of thing to say. They ought to be read differently because they ought to be heard differently. But in that magnificent old Gothic sanctuary, everything sounded like it was written in stained glass.

But the Bible is not a stained-glass book. On the contrary, it is a marvelously down-to-earth, uninhibited book—sometimes more so than we are comfortable with. There are, frankly, a lot of passages that we would be embarrassed to have read aloud in a worship service. Sometimes we are also embarrassed by how frank God is in the Bible. If anyone should seem as pristine and refined as stained glass, we reckon, it is God. Yet God claims to be jealous (Exodus 34:14), gets angry (2 Kings 17:18), regrets decisions (Genesis 6:6; 1 Samuel 15:35), and changes his mind (Exodus 32:14). Is this the stuff of holy perfection? It doesn't seem to fit, and so we chalk these instances up to anthropomorphisms by ancient writers, and we hurry on our way.

Identifying anthropomorphisms in the Bible—those instances where the writer gives God human characteristics so that we can more easily understand—isn't an exact science, however. As soon as Scripture reports that God made humankind in his image, it becomes a challenge to know who is being like whom. Is God portrayed in a certain way because of the human authors projecting what they are like onto God? Or could it be that we behave and feel a certain way because we are made to be like God?

The unblinking testimony of Scripture is that God is not static. God is not unchanging in the sense of being always in the same mood or always doing the same thing. Yet that doesn't mean that the Lord is capricious or unreliable. Rather, it reaffirms the fundamental truth that God is personal and relational.

We were created to be in relationship with our Creator. That is why we were made free. That is why Jesus revealed to us that what is most important—the "first and greatest commandment"—is that we should love God (Matthew 22: 37-38 NIV). But as soon as we affirm that God is in relationship with us, we recognize the possibility that we may affect God, just as God affects us. We can make the Lord pleased or sad, impressed or disappointed. And so God is not static.

Always Changing in the Same Direction

To say that God feels a variety of emotions, regrets certain choices, or even changes his mind is not disputing God's unchanging nature. Quite the contrary. A closer evaluation of those vacillations actually reinforces the fundamental and unchanging nature of God.

Consider, for example, the cases in which the Bible reports that God changed his mind. Most famously, the Lord threatens to destroy the chronically disobedient Israelites and start fresh with Moses and his descendants. Moses intercedes on behalf of the people, and "the Lord changes his mind" (Exodus 32:14; see also Deuteronomy 9).

Less familiar but equally significant is the testimony of Amos. The Lord shows Amos two visions of destruction (Amos 7:1-6). Amos interceded on behalf of the people both times. And both times "the LORD changed His mind" (7:3, 6 NASB).

In a similar vein, a few reflective people in Jeremiah's day remembered an earlier generation that had heeded the Lord's warnings through the prophet Micah. "Did Hezekiah king of Judah and all Judah put him to death?" they asked. "Did he not fear the LORD and entreat the favor of the LORD, and the LORD changed His mind about the misfortune which He had pronounced against them?" (Jeremiah 26:19 NASB). The stories involving Moses and Amos are both in the moment, while this passage from Jeremiah is recalling an earlier event. But the thrust of all three episodes is the same: the Lord changes his mind about punishing his people.

In the situations with both Moses and Amos, God had expressed his intent to bring destruction on the people. When the human servants of God speak up on behalf of the people, however, God relents. It is a lovely and powerful image of intercession. And it reflects a trajectory that we see again in the New Testament, where Jesus tells a parable about an unfruitful fig tree. The landowner in the parable laments to his servant one day, "See here! For three years I have come looking for fruit on this fig tree, and still I find none. Cut it down! Why should it be wasting the soil?" (Luke 13:7). Yet the servant prevails upon his master, pleading for the tree: "Sir, let it alone for one more year, until I dig around it and put manure on it. If it bears fruit next year, well and good; but if not, you can cut it down" (Luke 13:8-9).

Moses and Amos function like the servant in Jesus' parable. In each case, the Master has declared a judgment upon the living thing that is not living up to its purpose. Yet the servants intercede with their Master, who demonstrates a great willingness to reconsider the judgment.

In contrast to those episodes, however, there is the strange case of Jonah. Everyone else in the story appears to be more responsive to God than the prophet of God, Jonah. And Jonah's story shows us another case of a people—in this case the city of Nineveh—whom God has planned to destroy. The people repent, and the Lord relents. The difference in this episode, however, is that the human servant is not interceding on behalf of the people. On the contrary, Jonah is eager to see their destruction, which he regards as their just deserts, and Jonah is expressly sorry to see them spared (Jonah 4:1-2).

Take the stories all together, and we see the consistent heart of God. The announcement of judgment in advance, as we've noted earlier, is its own kind of mercy. God doesn't decide and then do it; God decides and then predicts it. In most cases, this clearly provides an opportunity for the people to repent. And, perhaps in more cases than we realize, it also provides an opportunity for God's servants to intercede—to plead for the unfruitful fig tree, and then to redouble the efforts to make it fruitful in the year ahead. God's perfect will, after all, is that the trees should bear fruit, not that they should be cut down.

Finally, the occasions when the Lord does change his mind should be contrasted to those times when he does not. In the instances of Moses and Amos, the human servants wanted the people to be spared, and God spared them. In the case of Jonah, on the other hand, the human servant wanted the people to be destroyed, but God did not destroy them. God only changes his mind in one direction, you see—in the direction of forgiveness and redemption. As the old Communion liturgy says, "[His] property is always to have mercy."[19] God's nature is unchanging, and we see this once again through Jesus in the New Testament.

Judgment, Grace, and the Character of God

In the Last Supper discourse recorded by John, Jesus identifies himself as the vine to our branches. The metaphor carries so much meaning, as it speaks to the nature of our relationship with Christ as well as the purpose and produce of our lives. Naturally, the key to fruitfulness for the branch is to abide in the vine (John 15:4-5). Yet Jesus reveals an interesting logic with respect to those branches that do not abide in the vine.

On the one hand, Jesus warns that the Father "cuts off every branch in me that bears no fruit" (15:2 NIV). On the other hand, Jesus explains which branches are the ones that bear no fruit: "No branch can bear fruit by itself; it must remain in the vine" (v. 4 NIV). Consequently, "If you remain in me and I in you, you will bear much fruit.... If you do not remain in me, you are like a branch that is thrown away and withers; such branches are picked up, thrown into the fire and burned" (vv. 5-6 NIV).

In this parable, we are presented with several images of judgment: branches being cut off, branches being thrown away, and branches being thrown into a fire. Yet which branches are the ones subject to such judgment? Those that do not bear fruit. And which branches do not bear fruit? Those that do not remain connected to the vine. We see, then, a cause-and-effect relationship suggested by Jesus' teaching. The branches that are "judged" are those branches that have not stayed connected. Put another way: the idea is that the Lord cuts off the branches that have first cut themselves off from the Lord. The judgment of God, then, is only an extension of the human choice.

If that is true, it is a dramatic assertion to make about the judgment of God. So far from impulsive, God's judgment is altogether predictable. And, to an extent, we might even say that God's judgment is within our control. That's not to say that we are stronger, or that we are in charge. It is to affirm that God is so constant—and so gracious—that divine judgment can be avoided, for God only cuts off the branches that have already cut themselves off.

In truth, the pattern we are exploring here is not a hard science. Perhaps we should leave aside, therefore, the language of cause and effect and think, instead, in terms of initiation and response. For the real picture here is of a relationship, and relationships are lived out in acts of initiation and acts of response—or, as the case may be, the absence of initiation or the absence of response.

We will understand the heart and character of God more fully, as well as our relationship with God, if we are clear about the pattern of initiative and response. Judgment, you see, is not an act of God's initiation. Judgment is only a response. And, as we have demonstrated, it is a reluctant response, at that. What is clear through both testaments is that God has an overwhelming desire to have a relationship with us, and that the open-arms invitation to repent and abide with God is ever present.

Running Hot and Cold

At this moment, it is 17 degrees Fahrenheit in Green Bay, Wisconsin, where I live. I am able to call up the weather details of other places around the world, and I discover that other people's situations are quite different from mine at this moment. It is 85 degrees in Cairo and 45 degrees in Oslo. It is 100 degrees in New Delhi, 36 degrees in Moscow, 77 degrees in Johannesburg, and 84 degrees in Perth.

Such variations do not surprise us, as we are quite accustomed to the news of widely varying temperatures around the globe. And yet, as familiar as the phenomenon is, perhaps there should be some surprise in it for us. After all, the people of both Wisconsin and India, of both Norway and

Australia, all function under the same source of heat—the sun.

Scientists tell us that the Earth is about 93 million miles from the sun. And that the sun, so very hot and so very far away, is our planet's source of heat—as well as our source of light. Is Green Bay that much farther from the sun than New Delhi that I should be shivering while they are sweating? No, the difference between us in terms of distance from the sun is so negligible as to be inconsequential. Yet given that we are essentially the same distance from our mutual source of heat, why are they so much warmer than I am?

We remember from our earliest science classes the models that we saw (and perhaps even tried to make) reflecting the components of our solar system. We learned about the relation of the various planets to the sun, as well as our own planet's tilt, rotation, and orbit. We were taught about the equator and the poles, about varying hours of sunlight, the equinoxes, and the dramatic variations in climate across the surface of the Earth.

The sun, meanwhile, remains constant. Well, *almost* constant, for astronomers warn that it will burn out in 5 billion years or so, so that's something to worry about. And we sometimes read about periodic solar flares and the potential disruption they can cause on Earth. But for the most part, human beings experience the sun as the very model of constancy—its rising in the morning in the east and setting in the afternoon in the west is a metaphor for all that is predictable and reliable. For the sake of argument, therefore, let us agree that the sun remains constant.

The sun is constant, but we can change our interaction with it. One person stays indoors, for example, and his skin becomes pasty. Another is out working and playing in the sun, and her skin turns tan. Another is outside, too, but without taking any precautions, and he gets burned. Despite how we interact with it, the sun is unchanging.

Like the sun, God is unchanging. God does not run hot and cold; we do. We human beings cannot do anything to make God less bright or less warm. But we can—and we do—make choices that dramatically impact our experience of that unchanging nature. Thankfully, our God remains the same, constantly guiding us back to the truth and the light.

The End of the Matter

In *The West Wing* episode we considered in the second chapter of this book, President Bartlet boasted that he was "more of a New Testament man."[20] Ironically, the very writers who wrote the New Testament would have disputed both his premise and his preference. And Bartlet, with his narrow focus, is left with two frightening choices: an unreliable God or an unreliable revelation of God.

Centuries earlier, the skeptic Marcion, too, might have fancied himself as more of a New Testament man. He did eliminate the Old Testament from his Bible. Yet he also eliminated much of what we call the New Testament too.

And so, though he made a dramatic denial of the God of the Old Testament, he discovered that the line was not so neatly drawn between Malachi and Matthew.

Poor Senator Vinick, meanwhile, did not come either to Bartlet's inadequate peace or to Marcion's presumptuous heresy. He just gave up the struggle altogether. Eschewing the growing pains that inevitably come from wrestling with God and God's Word, Vinick gave up and walked away from both.

All three men represent sad surrenders, though. Neither the integrity of God nor the integrity of Scripture need to be sacrificed for the sake of our temporary comfort. Instead, our endeavor is not to recreate God in our image or to our liking, but to discover God. We need not try to shrink God to fit into our view but rather we must strive to expand our view in order to see, appreciate, and adore all that God is and how God reveals himself to us.

God is holy and loving, righteous and just. God is wise, compassionate, faithful, and provident. God has glory, power, splendor, and majesty. He is gracious, merciful, and slow to anger. God never changes but is the same yesterday, today, and forever.

The love of God includes jealousy, for true love is never indifferent about the beloved's affections. God's love, like God's holiness, is intolerant of sin. It is, after all, the nature of true love to desire what is best for the beloved, and both God's holiness and God's love seek to save us from sin.

God's holiness includes righteousness. God is righteous and desires righteousness. Justice is a function of God's righteousness, judgment is a function of God's justice, and justification is a natural extension of both God's righteousness and God's love.

As we've seen in the Old Testament, Israel's "home movies" record for us the activity of God among a chosen people. That chosen people was a nation with laws and borders, crime and punishment, allies and enemies.

We have in the New Testament an even more remarkable record of God's activity. For there we read about the Son of God's incarnate ministry in this world, which is followed by the Holy Spirit's powerful presence in the midst of his people—people who formed the church, which has no borders and a very different sort of an enemy. Through it all, the nature of God and the will of God never change. People sometimes change in relation to God, but God does not change.

Rumors are a dangerous business, especially when they are not true. I hope we have discovered together that the common rumor you and I have heard about God is not true. Rather, it is based upon misunderstandings—or at least a lack of understanding. My earnest hope, therefore, is that we are coming to a fuller understanding.

As we grow to understand better God's written word, it will become for us a much larger resource and a richer blessing. To get there, however, we may need to reverse what is the common process among so many folks. Rather than paring down the Bible into a small thing that fits all of my sensibilities, I should instead let myself grow into it. Rather than dismissing what I do not understand, I will embrace it. Rather than discounting what I do not like, I will wrestle with it. And in the process, I leave myself open to the Spirit teaching, growing, and leading me.

As we grow to understand better God's written word, we will accomplish the even more essential thing. We will grow to know and understand God better. We will see the seamless integration of God's heart, nature, will, plan, purpose, and activity. And as we grow in our understanding of God, we will grow in our love of God, which is most important of all.

> *Let those who boast boast in this, that they*
> *understand and know me, that I am the*
> *Lord; I act with steadfast love, justice, and*
> *righteousness in the earth, for in these things*
> *I delight, says the Lord.*
>
> *(Jeremiah 9:24)*

Notes

1. *The West Wing*, Sixth Season, Episode 620, "In God We Trust," accessed September 1, 2016, http://westwing.bewarne.com/sixth/620wetrust.html.

2. Ibid.

3. C. S. Lewis, *Reflections on the Psalms* (New York: Harcourt Brace Jovanovich, 1958), 121.

4. Paul K. Jewett, *God, Creation, and Revelation: A Neo-Evangelical Theology* (Grand Rapids: Eerdmans, 1991), 190.

5. Jonathan Edwards, "Sinners in the Hands of an Angry God," *20 Centuries of Great Preaching*, Vol. 3 , Clyde E. Fant and William M. Pinson, editors (Waco: Word, 1971), 63.

6. Thomas C. Oden, *The Living God: Systematic Theology: Volume One* (San Francisco: Harper & Row, 1987), 99.

7. William Sangster, *The Pure in Heart: A Study in Christian Sanctity* (Nashville: Abingdon Press, 1954), 32.

8. In the Old Testament Law, the understanding was that the average worshiper had no transaction beyond the altar of the Tabernacle, which was the first object inside the Tabernacle compound. Only the priests approached the Tent itself. And only the High Priest entered the Holy of Holies, and only on the holiest day of the year, the Day of Atonement. In the design of the Temple of the New Testament era, the building itself was surrounded by a series of courtyards, and those reflected a kind of graduated access to the Temple, and by implication to the presence of God.

9. Charles Wesley, "'Tis Finished! The Messiah Dies," *The United Methodist Hymnal* (Nashville: The United Methodist Publishing House, 1989), 282 , stanza 2.

10. Charles Wesley, "Come, O Thou Traveler Unknown," *The United Methodist Hymnal*, 386, stanza 4.

11. "Lovingkindess," *Oxford Dictionaries*, accessed September 1, 2016, http://www.oxforddictionaries.com /us/definition/american_english/lovingkindness. See also http://www.bible-researcher.com/chesed.html.

12. Isaac Watts, "Before Jehovah's Awful Throne," *The Evangelical Hymnal* (Harrisburg, PA: The Evangelical Publishing House, 1921), 8.

13. Charles Wesley, "Come, O Thou Traveler Unknown," *The Cyber Hymnal*, accessed September 1, 2016, http://cyberhymnal.org/htm/c/o/comeotho.htm.

14. Frederick W. Faber, "There's a Wideness in God's Mercy," *The United Methodist Hymnal*, 121.

15. Theodoret of Cyr, *Ancient Christian Commentary on Scripture, Old Testament XIV* (Downers Grove: InterVarsity, 2003), 2.

16. Leslie D. Weatherhead, *The Will of God* (Nashville: Abingdon Press, 1972), 28.

17. C. S. Lewis, *Mere Christianity* (New York: The Macmillan Company, 1958), 31.

18. Charles Wesley, "Soldiers of Christ, Arise," *The United Methodist Hymnal*, 513, stanza 2.

19. *The Methodist Hymnal* (Nashville: The United Methodist Publishing House, 1964), #830, prayer following "B. Holy, Holy, Holy".

20. "The West Wing," Sixth Season, Episode 620, "In God We Trust," accessed September 1, 2016, http://westwing.bewarne.com/sixth/620wetrust.html.